Traveling Show

By

Robert Edward Zucker

Traveling Show
Fancy Dancers and Rainbows
By Robert Edward Zucker

Front cover drawn from "Jefferson as Rip Van Winkle" by S. Eytinge, Jr. ("Every Saturday," February 18, 1871).
Back cover art of Santa Catalina Mountains. Front and back cover art and illustrations by Robert E. Zucker.
Clip art courtesy of Zedcor Graphics.

Copyright © 2013 BZB Publishing, Inc. First print edition, October 15, 2013
ISBN-10: 1-939050-03-0
ISBN-13: 978-1-939050-03-8

Published by BZB Publishing Inc.
P.O. Box 91317
Tucson, Arizona 85752

Internet: http://robert-zucker.com, http://emol.org
E-mail: publisher@emol.org

Printed in the United States of America by CreateSpace, an Amazon.com company.
Available for sale through Amazon.com, CreateSpace and other outlets.

Traveling Show

his is where the roaming Traveling Shows of the 15th Century still lives on.

In the 1400s, thousands of minstrels performed throughout medieval Europe. As they journeyed from town to town, these roaming groups of entertainers would sing, dance and perform in a Traveling Show.

These minstrels composed the lyrics to spin a story that captivated the crowd with their words and tunes.

They sang embellished tales of faraway or imaginary places, events and legends. They were the storytellers with the road shows of days gone by.

Depending on its size, the Traveling Show would have several actors or could be just a single wandering performer - the one man show.

The streets of Renaissance Europe would be filled with these musicians and entertainers performing both day and night. But, by 1700, minstrels and Traveling Shows became extinct.

Today, the Traveling Show is embodied in the entertainment circuit of traveling celebrities and musicians- roaming between venues or television shows. The Traveling Show spirit is also found in the street musicians who entertain on the sidewalk or in the subway.

Also, the Traveling Show is played out in the scenes and the people who pass through one's own life. We all encounter people who exert great influence on our own destiny. Through the eyes and words of a minstrel, this traveler's story is told.

1

These pages are from a collection of my minstrel stories from the 20th Century.

In 1969, at age 16, I started writing poetry and drawing people and places. Over several decades, and about 1,000 poems later, they became my lifeline to the past. Forty years later, they are still beacons to the future. When composed, they weren't meant to be a continuous story. It just happened. The words developed into their own stories that were molded over the years in symbols and imagery. This volume features a selection of those poems to tell this story.

I wrote about growing up and the lives of the people who passed by as I transitioned through high school, college and the real world. These same words followed me for decades. Unknowing at the time, the poems would develop an unwitting theme, or string of themes, that seem to bind the decades together into a story of more than just myself. Follow the words that weave around those themes as people come in and out of my life and see the reflections of your own life.

Everyone has his or her own Traveling Show. As we interact with the people we meet, their influences on our lives shape the way we grow and how we present ourselves to the world.

The people in these poems lived, and died, with their own Traveling Shows as they tried to reach for rainbows. Some never did finish that journey. Through their eyes, I wrote about their travels through life. Through my eyes, they became my own travels.

Each poem is a slice of life and chapter on it own. Most of the poems were shared with the people they were written about as they took their own Traveling Shows on the road. The poems also foretold my story as it unfolded. My comments at the end of each poem are written decades later when I decided to finally compile this volume.

These poems were spontaneously written, usually at one sitting, to reflect on the people, places and events around me at the time. The handwritten copies are scanned from the original writings. The typed poems are dictated through speech recognition software. All of the signed artwork and photographs are my originals. Renaissance images, where noted, are clip art. The poems are placed mostly in date order to reveal the entire story. The reoccurring symbols evolved into their own meanings as the poems progressed.

These pages are dedicated to all of the angels and fancy dancers who helped to inspire these words, and especially, to those who got lost along the way.

Now, I am able to tell my own minstrel story. These are the songs waiting to be sung.

> *I'm only a poem.*
> *A poem I'm meant to be.*
> *And as a poem*
> *I'm the story of me.*

Robert Zucker, 2013

"Be not forgetful to entertain strangers:

for thereby some have entertained angels unaware."

Hebrews 13:2 from the King James Bible

Artwork of the Angel Raphael, God Has Healed. Drawn about 1976.

Inside the Traveling Show

Artwork of a traveler, drawn in pencil on October 9, 1973 at age 19 in the midst of my journey.

TRAVELING SHOW

#463
Nov. 20, 1974

Traveling on a rainbow
In hopes to reach the sun.
A piece of sky, piece of dream
Angels across the heavens.

Treading the waters by the riverside
Collecting flowers that grow near by.
The wind seems to sweep me away
Blowing endlessly, past my eyes.

Am I a player in a traveling show
To amuse the audience for awhile.
Am I the seeker who lost his way
Paying for the people to smile.

For nickels and dimes I make my living
To be spent in a roundabout way.
Behind a grey wall of smoke I stand
To face the world each day.

When I look for some direction
Only the flames dances before my eyes.
And it leads me to keep wondering
If the river is just a bit too wide.

Have I been changing,
Rearranging
All my world to see
Have I lived in the memories
Of what I'm suppose to be

Am I a player in a traveling show
That entertains the simple souls.
Am I the seeker who lost his way.
A stranger who'll I'll never know.

Bob

Original handwritten copy. I often feel like I'm part of someone else's Traveling Show.

Traveling Show

*T*raveling on a rainbow,
In hopes to reach the sun.
A piece of sky, a piece of dream with angels across the heavens.

Treading the waters by the riverside.
Collecting flowers that grow nearby.
The wind seems to sweep me away.
Blowing endlessly past my eyes.

Am I a player in a Traveling Show,
To amuse the audience for a while?
Am I the seeker who lost his way,
Paying for the people to smile?
For nickels and dimes I make my living
To be spent in a round about way.
Behind it a gray wall of smoke I stand to face the world each day.

When I look for some direction, only the flame dances before my eyes.
And it leads me to keep wondering if the river is just a bit too wide.
Have I've been changing, rearranging all of my world to see?
Have I lived in the memories of what I'm supposed to be?
Am I'm a player in a Traveling Show
Who entertains the simple souls?
Am I the seeker who lost his way?
A stranger I'll never know.

#463 November 20, 1974, at age 24, halfway through this poetic journey, I realize I'm a Traveler, too.

Discovering the World
Through the Words of a Poem

I began to explore the world around me as a teenager through words- journals and poetry. My earlier poems, written in the 1960s and early 1970s, examined mankind's treatment of the world, humanity and many of the deep pondering issues faced in adolescence, especially as the country was struggling with war.

Photo: Holding a lucky catch off the coast in California, June 1970.

The Dream

Dream about it all.
For what is here now
Will be gone tomorrow.
And with it all will be the dreams of
Yesterday's tears and sorrow.

A thought of someone
Will last only for a short time.
It will soon be forgotten
And pushed to the back of the mind.
Remind yourself of the good things in life.

For only happiness will help
To make things go right.

Don't let the past fade for only a tear will take the place
Of the fears that will invade memories that can't be retraced.

I hope your thoughts of me
And the past that we shared together
Will never cease to exist
For the dreams will still be there.

There's not much to remember me by
Except for the poems I left behind.
Just don't make the living past ever die
For it is imprisoned by our minds.

Thank you for the kindness you've shown.
And happiness you brought me each day.
And for making my life feel at home
Though my hopes are so far away.
I'll always remember the past.
It's a stepping-stone of what's to come.
For shadows of the future that have been cast
From dreams far beyond will forever shine on.
I'm writing this poem as an appreciation
And to all of my friends
Who have helped make my life shine.
Thank you.

#25 November 12, 1970. Written at age 16, when I begin to sort out the world ahead of me.
Artwork of "Good Spirits" drawn about 1974.

Secrets

G ather around and let me share
The wisdom I have recently learned.
Get comfortable as I tell you where,
And how, all this new experience has turned
Life into a circle game.

I've learned a secret only known to me.
I've seen what this secret can show and what it means.

Let me relate some experiences from the past.
It's not very important, but you'll see,
What it's done to make this secret last.
Trust me sincerely, as I trust you.
Don't let this secret get away. For only harm it will do.
Don't let this secret the stay deep inside of you.

Don't be fooled. It's not worth the pain to find out
About these secrets the hard and painful way.
But don't just wait and sit and watch the rain.

Now, I'll tell you what I know.
Just be careful and listen.
Then you can go and show
That this secret is about someone I know.

#42 November 17, 1970, age 16. Wrote this during high school, an eerie preface of what's to come.

Who can tell?

*A*nd so the story goes of the man and the beast.
The hate and fighting between them never ceased.

Then one day, the man decided to get back at him.
He took a part of the tree and hit him with the limb.
The beast got mad and started to
explode.

Now comes the best part, as it is
told. The beast killed the man
and ruined his land.

He got so mad. Wherever he
went, everything was damned.

He left destruction upon the
earth and no one to be.
Many had died. No one lived.
The only thing alive was he.

That is like the story of the present day.
When this beast will destroy the world, no one can say.
When this beast does come, all will be known.
Who is this beast? It is the bomb.

#2 January 19, 1969, age 15. The Vietnam War and the struggles against the modern world.
Clip art of man being attacked by the tree beast, discovered in a clip art book 40 years later.

A Cry for Peace

Can anyone see the pain in me?
Can anyone see the hate done to me?
Born and condemned into a world of hate.
To begin with brother, it's too late.

We're shoved into a saddened society
Where man's last thought is of humanity.
Only to either do or to die,
This hate among men- I can't understand why.
If we could only correct this saddening thing,
Then peace throughout the land would give its ring.

We could then turn to Him, the Master, God,
Asking for peace and the golden rod.
He questions us, "Why all the hell and all the hate?"
Our answer lies in our present fate.
Thousands have lived and thousands have died
Protecting our land, and being our guides.

When I think of all the men of humanity
Who have sacrificed their lives for me,
If I could only thank them with God's grace,
For all their contributions to the human race.
But look at the situation we're in,
Hating our neighbor, because of his skin.
There must be a better way to work for peace,
All of this hate and fighting must cease.

The call is heeded, over and over.

Knock off that dope and stay sober.
Stop that fighting among fellow men,
We'll show this world, time and again.
Let us feed the hungry, and help the poor.

We must stop the killing.
We must end the wars.
Love one another, before it's too late,
Bring in the love, and throw out the hate.
We must do it before we disintegrate.

We have to give it at least one try,
Before we all say our final goodbye.

January 16, 1969. One of my first poems, at age 15, won 3rd in the United Nations Poetry Contest, 1969.
"A Cry for Peace," May 6, 1969, one of my first drawings at age 15, influenced by the Vietnam conflict.

In The Beginning

*I*n the beginning, God created heaven and earth.

The land was unformed and barren. And God said;

"Let the earth be green and fruitful."

And the earth was green and fruitful. And it was good.

And God said; "Let there be people to enjoy this green and fruitful earth."

And there were people. He saw the people. And it was good.

And the people lived upon the land and worked.

They were born and died upon the land for centuries.

And God watched over His children.

He watched them work and play, love and hate, live and die, kill and pollute.

Soon, the green lands became brown from poisons sprayed by the animal,

Man, to ward off unwanted beasts.

The blue oceans became black from gushes of oil killing fish and plants.

The clear blue sky became dirty and toxic from wastes that man had poured into it.

These supreme beings that God had created

Took the power of life and death into their own hands, and

Destroyed the green and fruitful land God gave them to live upon.

And God said; "My children, why must you destroy this beautiful world I have given you?"

But His children did not answer for they thought He was dead.

And finally, the earth was destroyed by ball of fire

Formed by one man who called himself God.

1969, written around the same time "A Cry for Peace," my self-discovery phase as a teenager.

18

Keep the Faith

When they say the end is near
No outlook for tomorrow.
Just keep the faith
There's more to follow.

When the water's so polluted, you choke 'til you're dead
And the sky's so filthy you cough 'til you're red,
And, when the Bomb wipes us out and the Pill cuts us down,
Drugs blow our minds while the skies stay brown.

When the forests are gone and buildings leave no view,
We'll sit back in our easy chair wondering what to do.
While half the world starves before they go to bed,
Men fight for our country, now living and dead.

Just keep the faith and press ahead.
Let's not give in before we're all dead.

When a radicals voice preaches corruption
And man's environment falls to destruction
People smoke up on a stick of grass
Trying to make the evils of the world pass.

When money's our God and they say He's dead
Hate's brought against the Black, Yellow and Red.
People riot to change unjust laws.

But no one listens to their useless calls.

Just keep the faith and open your eyes.

Don't become blind to all the lies.

While inflation's high and quality's low,

And in the place of forests, cities grow.

If man resorts to guns to gain his peace.

Then the threat of war will never cease.

Let's just keep the faith, try to understand.

Let's not give up, just give a damn.

And if we have faith while we're still around ,

We'll bury the hatchet beneath the ground.

From the rays of hope, bringing the light of peace.

The hate and troubles burdening us may cease.

Just keep the faith, or what's meant will be.

Unless man changes the course of his destiny.

#21 September 18, 1970, age 16. Kent State, Jackson State Shootings and the conflicts overseas.

Words of a poem

Pages of books
Strewn around the room
Of stories someone once had written.

Now lie crumbled, torn and burned.
Words that have lost their meaning.

He throws a glass against the wall.
It shatters into a million pieces.
Each piece tells the story of
A thousand broken dreams.

The woman pushes back her curly hair.
Seems she's getting a little bit older.

Losing their senses of what to do.
Loneliness sets in when time gets longer.

And are you so happy you lived so long.
Wasting your whole life into words of a poem.
The man shakes his head. What else is he going to do?
Pages of lines written to read.
The story of another man's world.

Written in 1972, age 18, my fears of the future and how they are embodied in the words of a poem.
Photo of these poems spread around my library 40 years later as I compile this volume.

My first experience

*T*he sky was still dark.
The moon was high.
We were alone, her and I.

Her hair was brown. Her eyes were blue.
I knew just what I had to do.

To do it with courage, to do it my best.
I placed my hand upon her breasts.

My hand was steady. Her body was fine.
I ran my hand down her spine.

I trembled and shook. I felt her heart.
And I carefully spread her legs apart.
I knew she was ready.
But I didn't know how.
It was my first experience
In milking a cow.

April 1, 1969. Learning about the farm from a high school friend.

Shepherd

Wishing on a dream that will never come true.
The old man looks over the countryside.
High above humanity, deep in the hills
He watches the sun slowly slip from the sky.

Gathered around him, his flock grazes.
Gnawing at the grass until it finally gives away.

Old man, you are a shepherd among the men
Gracing your fields for another day.
Ripples of time line your mind.
Your hair reflects the years gone by
And the centuries you've guided your sons
Who slowly pass your youthful eyes.

Age makes no difference. Time stands still.
After all of your children lived and died.
They will recall the story you played.
As a shepherd of eternal life.

September 1972, age 18, just after high school graduation. I had no idea of the flock I would attend.

Discovering Poems
Through Life's Experiences

Evolving from poetry about mankind, I begin to examine my own life and the people who pass through. These poems, written in high school, covered a period of transition from moving back to my hometown after a near ten-year absence. What I left behind became apparent as I sharpened my poetry themes to become a traveler in my own universe.

In 1971, at age 17, a rare occasion to wear a suit.

25

Déjà vu

*C*reated with a new light shining on me.
Conceived by dreams from ashes
Returning again for me to see.

My life is being formed and made from the illusions of memories.
Déjà vu. I remember you.
I can see the world through their eyes.
I can touch the material things that are to soon form my life.
And I can sense the visions of pureness that put Heaven in the skies.

All this seems so much to me.
Yet, I know I have been here before.

All this is familiar that I see.
But only dreams are still here.

There's a new feeling running through my hands that lets me experience my existence.

It changes the beginning over again.
I can open my eyes and breathe the air.
I can change my thoughts to happiness
Because my heart has grown near
To the creation of a new life
Of the things I see, the words I hear.

I leave the darkness of unknown left behind.
Seeing a lighter light shining on me.

New illusions my spirit can find
To either help or hinder my future.
These are the dreams of my mind.

Déjà vu, I remember you.

#44 November 19, 1970, age 16. Returning home, remembering old friends.
Artwork of the mountains against the farm land, drawn October 27, 1968, before leaving for home.

Gone

H iking down the lonely country roadside.

Sun beating upon my head, wind against my face.

Watching the cars pass by, trying to hitch a ride.

My belongings on my back, left without a trace.

Four days on the road, a dollar to my name.

Sleeping outside with nature under the stars.

Footprints left in the mud from last night's rain.

So close to my destination, yet so far.

Please help me through this coming day.

Protect me from the darkness of night.

Help me help myself, see me on my way. I pray my decision was right.

There's so much to see in this large world. The thousands of cities, they're all mine.

But, as I wander with no place to go,

Wandering by myself, I'm all alone.

I don't know what's ahead of me.

So many places to go, now that I left home. A world of strangers for me to meet.

Rambling on in search of nothing, town after town,

My stomach is hungry, my body fatigued.

But, I'm not going to stop. I have to go on.

Please help me through this coming day.

Protect me from the darkness of night.

Help me help myself. See me on my way.

I pray my decision was right.

#46 November 27, 1970. This is the story of the Travelers, told to me several years later.

A Rainy Day

Rays of a rainbow march across the heavens.
Beads of color produced by the sun.
Dark clouds break apart the sky to let the sun's warmth pass by.
Droplets of rain form puddles on the ground. Pieces of the sky fallen down.

I walk outside and my arms embrace the rain that has fallen on my face.
As I look up at the cloudy skies raindrops splattered in my eyes.
I opened my mouth and let the rain fall in.
The freshness of nature makes me grin. I just love a rainy day.
Its serenity takes me away to distant dreams in distant lands
Where time falls in grains of sand.

The morning showers awaken the sky.
The rain washes the earth, not a spot left dry.
A chill runs through my body from a blowing breeze.
Shining beads of water collect upon green leaves.
A darkness surrounding me as the rain trickles down.
The beat of the raindrops makes a continuous sound.

A smell of freshness as showers pass by.
A break in the clouds shows the deep blue sky.
There's a certain feeling that comes with the rain
 It's a sensation that can't be explained.
A walk in the rainy darkness of night. All the raindrops that form my life.
Remnants of the storm that has passed. Glistening rainbows that have been cast.

#48 November 6, 1970. It rarely rains in California or the Arizona desert. Each shower cleanses.

It's only a dream

*T*he world around you is just dream.

All of the images of life seen are just games in your head.

All that's been done and said is not real to anyone except you.

The good and
the bad turn
happiness from sad.

As the dreams form
in your mind

And the visions
that define

As you enjoyed your
eternal sleep, see those
dreams play little games.

Watch them all
As they decide the way
your life is going to be
for you and for me.

And, see if they are real.

The sounds that are heard and the images made
Can make a person believe
That life is such a reality.
 Dream it, and see if it's true.

#51 December 10, 1970. Images from my aquarium and dreams fused into one.
Panels 1, 2 and 3 of Artwork, "Angel fish and angels in waiting," drawn in the late 1970s.

Light a candle in the window

I am heading home as I wander down the road.
The night is getting chilly. My body is cold.
My hands in my pocket as I kick the ground.

The lonely call of an owl is the only sound.
For years I wandered. I had no place to go.
For all of my life I had nothing to show.

I close my eyes while I'm heading home.
The vision of your face on my mind.

Light a candle in the window
I'll be home tomorrow.
It's glowing flame
Will restore my dreams.

#49 December 9th 1970. Leaving the ocean for a return back home. I am the traveler.

Reflections

*L*ooking back, what is it I see.
Reflections of the past behind me.
A year of joy, a year of sorrow
Starts a new beginning tomorrow.

Are there dreams looking ahead?
Are there hopes that are to be spread?
To a brighter future to see across a lifetime to eternity.

Peeking over the horizon
A new sun is rising as I turn my head.
The sun isn't there, only a new life me to begin.
Only an old one for me to end.
Reflections that show what has passed.
A slice of life in a memory will last.
The happiness that has come.
From the sadness that is gone.

#62 December 27, 1970. I know what has passed will only push me ahead. Time to pack my bags.

As the cold wind blows

I am heading south. I'm leaving home.
All the dreams I've had are now gone.
All that I lived for is washed away.

I just can't stay here another day.
I'm not leaving anything behind.
I'm going to take all that's mine.
All I have left is shattered dreams
And the years that mean so much to me.
I watched the cold wind blow

And with it all my dreams go.
Blowing across the land
Settling into fields of grain
To be washed away
With the coming rains.

If I have something the live for
I'd never want anything more.

I take with me my silent tears
I had within myself all these years.

I watch the cold wind come my way
And with it go the clouds of grey.

As I go, she'll never know
That I really loved her so.

#67 January 2, 1971, age 16, I left behind more than my heart in San Francisco.
Artwork of Reddington Pass near Tucson, April 1974; and portrait of a real angel drawn February 1971.

Shadows

He was a traveling minstrel
Who never knew his home.
Roaming from town to town
Spreading his music around.

He wandered down the lonely country roads.
Along each stop he composed his poems.
Each night he camped with rambling men.
He would tell his story time and again.
As they gathered around a campfire light,
His voice would flow out, haunting the night.
He shared the stories of a blind man's need.
When he spoke, every living soul would heed.
Every eye watched upon his hands.
His eyes met upon every man.
Each heart would be filled with sorrow
As they carried their dreams till tomorrow.

When they awaken from the morning
They find the minstrel gone in the night.
If it's more tears they want,
They'll seek him once more.
And they'll hearken to his tales as they did before.

#88 February 27, 1971. I was to become a minstrel as I continued to gather my words in poems.

This Old House

*D*ust falls as the table taps
As the shutters begin to creak.
The wind howls through the house
As the old mansion silently sleeps.

Books line the shelves of wood as cobwebs cover the doorway.
Quiet footsteps walk each night as this old house stands each day.
No one's entered and no one's left. The old house door's been bolted for years.
Dusk falls upon its fading walls. Each night, the house fills with fears.

Through the darkness of eve
Shadows crawl upon the floors.
The house creaks with age
With the sounds of slamming doors.

Hell has no fury with this house.
It's been empty for years.
With the murder of the owner
Upon its gold winding stairs.

The house creaks in the dark
The eyes follow a moving light
With the haunting sounds of death
As the body rises each night.

#96 March 14, 1971. Every home tells a story, like the Winchester Mansion. Some are haunted.
Clip art of an old mansion.

Rosy cheeks

"*How will I recognize you?*
Tell me, what will you wear?
What you do want me to do
To let you know I'm here?"

"*My hair is made of flowing gold.*
My face is white as snow.
My lips whisper the story that's told
Of what my innocence shows.

"*My nose is small and dainty.*
For I am the one you seek.
With eyes as blue as clear skies,
I am the girl with rosy cheeks.

"*Rosy cheeks will place me where I can be found.*
Rosy cheeks describe me from my head to the ground.
Rosy cheeks are hidden undercover to protect from warm and damp.
Rosy cheeks will be discovered at Simon Floop's Nudist Camp."

#101 March 23, 1971. Teenage years are a time for exploration in poetry.

Who is she?

Who is she?
Her life is so
Mysterious to me.

Her world is secluded.
Her thoughts are eluded.
Her happiness is excluded.

An image transparent
Is all that I see.
Nothing is apparent. Who is she?

Never a word of happiness
Only sorrow.
Just silence across her face.
What are her hopes for tomorrow?
What dreams take her place?

If I could probe and see
What will I find?
Who is she?
Her silence seems like a call.
I need an answer to satisfy me,
To tell me what I'm searching for.
Who is she?

#104 April 15, 1971 at age 17. She was so mysterious that I was drawn to her.
"Ecstasy, the Empire Lady" Artwork, December 1974.

San Francisco Fog

T he beauty of San Francisco on a foggy day
    Feeling droplets of water wash my face
    A cool breeze blowing through the air
Running free in the fog without care.

Golden Gate Park so damp and so wet
From the daily morning fog that met
San Francisco on a breezy spring day.
As a sun comes to push the fog away
Clouds of haze block my view
Filling the air with morning dew.
Blocking off the rest of life
Making the day as grey as night.

Can't see the world beyond my hand.
Can't see beyond the bay island.
Alcatraz disappears in the sky
As the Golden Gate Bridge hides its face.

The rolling hills of city streets
Gone from the sight as they meet
The sky that seems to end so near
That repeats itself throughout the year.

Calls of sea gulls like fog horns
Letting out a continuous sound.
Cable cars find their way in the dark

People sleeping out in Golden Gate Park.

Market Street is busy is ever
As San Francisco fades into forever.
The beach is silent, houses stand underneath the forgotten sky.

By noon, the bay is dry and clear.
No more droplets forming in my hair.
No more dampness on the ground
No more grey fog to be found.

#119 May 6, 1971. My memories shared with the mysterious woman who never visited San Francisco.
SF Golden Gate Bridge drawn October 1971.

Never again

We lead our dreams
Into tears of sorrow.
And let those tears
Carry us on to tomorrow.

We left our hearts
In the corners of our minds.
And we let our dreams
Fade away with time.

We gave our souls
Into false entities.
And let our hearts
Take away our dreams.

#174 May 8, 1972, age 18. The burden of carrying those burdens over 174 poems later.

Artwork of "Greece on the Ruins of Missolonghi," drawn in 1976 from painting by E. Delacroix, 1826

Flowers

O nce a lonely flower stood
With its leaves wilted
And dying.

No one around

To give it comfort.

They just left it crying.

Then upon a warm spring day

Another flower bloom by its side

Talking of things and falling in love

They began to share a life.

Both bloomed towards the sun.

They raised their petals high

And the earth around them

Felt the warmth of their smiles.

Sun shines and sun sets.

Each day they lived through

Like the summer sun reaching its rays

To drive up the morning dew.

Soon as the seasons passed on

The flowers seemed to change.

And as strange as it seems

Neither flower was to blame.

And one flower asked
Why must we both wilt this way?
Is it the ground drying up
Or other things that took its place.

So as the flowers wilt and die
Nobody is left to water them
No one even questions why
Beautiful flowers must wilt again.

#204 November 9, 1972. Thinking about a high school sweetheart who I thought was going stay.
Artwork of a rose, November 23, 1971.

Isn't it time

Darkness starts to encumber me while lady death waits by my side.
Pictures of my past turned into dreams
As my life slowly slips by.

Isn't it time to make my plans.
Time to say goodbye.
Shouldn't I leave peacefully.
Isn't it time for me to die.

Stepping into tranquility
Visions seem to just fade away.
They call out for me to answer.
But, I have nothing to say.

Feeling a tear fall on my cheek
From someone standing above me.
She grasps my hand, holding it tight.
She was once a memory.
We took a walk one summer day
Into a field of grass and trees.
Then, she told me she had to go.
Don't you know, it just had to be.

Now, she stands and sheds a tear
After so many years of sorrow.
Crying of dreams of yesterday.

But, I won't be here tomorrow.

A voice tells me I'm almost gone.
But I only hear an echo.
As I enter the world of peace, I let my whole life go,

Someone is mumbling a prayer to send my soul to heaven.
Another tear falls upon my face to wash away all my sins.

I had no wishes to depart.
But also had no wishes
To die of a broken heart.

#201 September 16,1972 at age 18. The end of one's life, or a relationship, is only the start of another.

Traveling Down the Road

Graduation from high school and the start of college was more than a classroom education. This journey brought encounters with many passer-bys who came in and out of my life, returning many times with tales of their own Traveling Shows.

Self-portrait drawn September 1972, just after high school graduation.

Sunset Daydreams

I guess the sun set for one last time.
It's so sad to see it go away.
But the sun can't last forever.
It only stays for just a day.

Traveling down a long dark road
With so many thoughts behind me.

Guess it's time to find a new home.
Guess it's time to discover new dreams.
And someone asked, why so sad?

Don't you know,
I just can't explain.

I said it was cloudy outside.
Whenever it's cloudy, it rains.

She nodded her head,
Although she knew
She could see it in my eyes,
Tell it in my soul.

But, what could I say,
I traveled on.
With my books in hand,
I look for home.

And then, someone tapped me
On the shoulder

And said, please come with me.
Let's start a brand new page.
Let us rewrite to your history.

#208 November 11, 1972. While graduation ended one cycle, another one is to begun.
Sunset Daydreams Artwork, 1972.

Only a Poem

I am only a poem, to be seen in many ways.
Like a picture in a storybook.
Like a line from a play.

I am only a poem.
I could be torn in shreds.
Thrown out with the trash
Left dying with the dead.

I am only a poem
Like the lines on a page.
I can be erased from the paper.
I can be changed like the days.

I am only a poem.
Someone put me in a book
And exposed my meanings
So everyone can look.

I am only a poem.
A poem I am meant to be.
And just like a poem
I am the story of me.

#210 November 15, 1972. After two hundred poems, I began to think like a poem.
Photos from 1972, high school at age 18.

Flowing Well

Ocean breeze steps before me and keeps me traveling in time.
Grains of sand around my toes.
Each piece of earth is mine.

Someone claimed my land.
Built a town, dug a well.
On holidays they rang a bell.

Someone stood by the well
asking for a cup to drink.
Strange to me, no one could see.
Didn't even stop to think.

The well was drained one
cloudy day from a drink that
would never end.

Each person took an endless turn until the well was drained.
Then a trickle of water had filled the well again.
It took its time, but it was done.
An internal flow to an internal end.

One town had risen, one had fallen. But the well remained the same.
The plants around had used its flow to keep them living without rain.
And with sands of time the town had changed.
But the flowing well just stayed the same.

#220 December 20, 1972. Conquistadors took away the lands, but they couldn't take away the water.
California ocean side photograph, circa 2008.

Traveling on the road

S itting in a roadside café. A cup of coffee in my hand.
It's 3a.m. it's getting late.
Maybe I should hit the road again.

Weather's cold, should button up
This tattered coat I'm wearing.
Too bad I'm here all alone,
With no dreams to be sharing.

Look ahead, a dime to my name.
Must be better place to be.
Thought I once found a better way.
Found out I was only fooling me.

Shook my head to keep awake.
Maybe I should still go on.
But how much more can I take
As I move from town to town.

Country music in my ears from a corner
store nearby. Stopped in, gave him a dollar
for some food to get me by.

The sun is peeping from behind
The mountain peaks around me.
As the sky lights up, shines in my eye
I can begin to smell the salty sea.

Blue ocean on my mind, but so far away.

As the sand curls around my toes,

Guess it will take just one more day to find a place to call home.

Hitching along a country road waiting for cars to pass.

Lost the first one, the second one slowed.

But the third stopped to give me a ride.

We talked of life and things we've done

And passed a few hours away.

As the sun beat down to warm the ground

We kept on driving through the day.

Never knew his name or who he really was

Except for what I saw in my eyes.

Then I looked at all I've done

We traveled on through the night.

He left me by a town nearby a bus station for me to sleep in.

Put some dollars in my hand. I thanked him twice.

Said he'd hoped we'd meet again.

Slept the day, waiting for the plane

That never made it to the station.

Walked the streets, still felt the same

Not knowing where I've been.

Traveling on a road in search of a dream.

Looking in every town I've been.

Funny feeling the inside of me.

I guess I'll hit the road again.

#227 December 26, 1972. Her tale was that of a traveler who kept coming back.
Mt. Lemmon road photo, 1978.

Poems without lines

I write a poem.
Seems like I've done before.
Suddenly there's no meaning
Or else it means that much more.

I looked down from my pen.
Seems like my paper is still blank.
With two more cups of coffee
Near the one I just drank.

And dreams with no meaning.
A poem without any lines.
A storm without an umbrella.
A penny without a dime.

Staring into an empty cup
With no thoughts on my mind.
Waiting for another coffee.
Writing a poem without lines.

#241 January 16, 1973. Sometimes, there's just no words.

Sail Away

When the evening falls
The sun hides its face.
I walk out in the daylight
Hoping to find the place.

I ran into the darkness. It covered my soul.
I watched the star dust as it became my home.

I looked for an exit. Seems there's no way out.
Looked at the emptiness, I watched in doubt.

Come down by the ocean, and watch me sail away.
Watch me drown my sorrow into the filthy bay.

Fifty million people watched me sail away.
Waving goodbye at the dock
They watched me fade away.

#245 January 17, 1973. Everyone steers their own ship of fools.

Monday Morning

Sitting Monday morning
A coffee cup to my right.
Crackling of bacon grease
Scrambled eggs on the side.

A smile from the morning sun.
Spring singing in the trees
Like dew on the frosty grass
And flowers swaying in the breeze.

Reading the morning paper. Checking the classified ads,
Turning to the obituaries. Reflections from a broken glass.

Shattered teardrops come sparkling to be blown away by the wind.
To be gathered and tossed away. God knows where they've been.

Who's to complain of the rain if it's not falling anywhere else.
Just as long as the sun shines
It'll only be falling on myself.
A cup of coffee in my hand is getting cold to even drink.
Guess it's time to spill it out.
Time to begin a new dream.

#254 February 1, 1973. My life becomes full of passing minstrels with their own stories and songs.

Traveling Ladies

There were several traveling ladies with their own stories to tell. They lived by the rules of the open road- mostly of their own design. These poems were shared with them as they revolved through my life.

Gypsy of the bar room stands

The lady is gone, gone for the night,
Leaving behind her flock of men.
And as she goes, one follows her home.
She's the gypsy of the bar room stands.

No one knows her,
Yet she's always there.

Entertaining the men
In all her splendor.
Polishing them off, she smiles on.

Fancy clothes donned with jewelry.
Golden hair falls down by her side.
Every one says she's a good number,
They all stayed with her for the night.

From honkytonks and two bit joints.
Each and every dawn she's weaving.
A golden web to catch her prey
Each and every night she's receiving.

She's known by all in every hall.
She's always there, waiting in the night.
Then, when one o'clock comes around
She's singing her song of delight.

By sunrise her lover is up and gone.
And she's left to be all alone
Until night time comes around again.
For halls and bars are all she's ever known,

And she lies in her bed with tears in her eyes.
Something she's so used to feeling.
And don't you know what her troubles are-
It's all those years that everyone is stealing.

A faded photograph in her snow white hands.
Clouded by the many tears in her eyes
Of someone she once new long ago.
Now faded into the memories of her life.

She's the Gypsy of the bar room stands
For everyone wants to be her lover.
And into the night she slips away
Into the arms of another.

#276 March 1,1973. For all of the Gypsies out there.
Clip art of a fancy dancer.

Pages of Life

*A*nd doesn't it seems so funny
That we should meet again
Behind tall walls of memories
And changes we have lived.

And it's the pages of life turning
Through the episodes of my mind.
Just looking back and returning
To see what memories
I may find.

#295 March 25, 1973. The cycle continues, pages start accumulating. Friends stop back for a while.
Photo booth picture of Beth and Keli, 1973.

Rainbow

Smiling like a rainbow.
Colors across
the sky.

Brightening up
the saddest face.

Opening up the
widest eyes.

Glistening like a rainbow.

Displaying all her rays.

Into each heart she enters
to block away the rain.

#307 March 28,1973. Sometimes, rainbows still appear when least expected.
Clip art of a king and queen dining across a rainbow.

The Past

A faded photograph
Once images of the past
Of what once used to be
Now faded memories.

A scrapbook with worn pages
People with smiling faces.
Just pages of reflections
Of lost expectations.

Letters yellow from sands of time
Poems written in so many lines
Seems to bring back lost tears
Of love faded through the years.

#321 April 10,1973. She was there- and then, she wasn't.
Photo on the porch, circa 1975.

Highway

I *don't want to say I'm traveling.*
Though I don't know where I am.
Just gone too many miles.
Traveled down too many roads.

And I wonder where I'm going
No direction which to travel
Only detours turn me around
To start all over again.

Down the long highway
Everyone calls their home
So many alleys to fall in
It's wonder I don't get lost.

#342 June 14, 1973. She took to the highway in search of the road, hoping to find a pot gold.

Home Again

W alking down the quiet streets
       Of what used to be my home
       Familiar, yet so strange to me
Memories I used to know.

It feels so good to be here
There is so much I left behind
And thinking brings a happy smile
Of all of things that once were mine.

And I'm back home.

Just for a while.

I'm not staying long.

I still got to travel.

There's a world I still want to see.

Part is now etched in my mind.

And its calls are beckoning me

To the freedom I must find.

#334 May 13, 1973 at age 19. I'm going back to another home for the summer. The farm I once visited.

Artwork of a friend's horse stable in the mountains, San José, CA, 1971.

Photo of the same spot a few years later.

Full Moon Night

*S*it around the campfire and see the moon.
　　For it seems pretty full out tonight, I said,
　　As I opened up my eyes
And pointed my finger to the skies.

Lie in the grass and ease your mind.
Let's count the number of stars.

To them I told, the moon is very old
And the stars are so very far away.

My children, you look so peaceful
With the reflection of the lights
Shining in your eyes and faces
They seem so pure and white.

The moon once had a home
I whispered very softly
But, well enough, for all to hear
They listened while I spoke.
He lived right here on the earth
Deep beneath the blue ocean
Yet one day he got a mad
And never spoke to the earth again.

But, doesn't it seem lonely
Up there, so far in space.

I looked over to everyone
To watch the sadness in their face.

But forward, he continues
As the earth goes the other way.
And neither of them have spoken
Even to this very day.

That's why the moon wears a frown on his face
And shares a lonely star to his right
Who travels with him all alone
As they float through the darkness all night.

#355 July 17, 1973. Sometimes, relationships just don't work out, even among celestial beings.

Dancing clown

Fancy footwork across the stage,
    Amusing the people, he smiles.
    A song he sings, the banjo plays.
He sips from his bottle of wine.

The audience claps to his steps
As they toss him nickels and dimes.
A worn out hat and tattered clothes.
He winks his bloodshot eyes.

Dancing for the drunken crowd
That smells from beer and wine.
And every night the same old tale
In your empty glass tonight.

So sing a song and dance a line.

Seems your troubles are not yet found.
Put on a show for the people to see
As they call you the dancing clown.

#358 August 5, 1973. Watching the drunk acting like a clown at the bar- a modern day Mr. Bojangles.

Welcome Back

Sitting by the window sill
Waiting for your return.
Counting the cars passing by
Waiting to see you again.

Spider crawls across the window
Hurrying to get home.
And I'm sitting in my chair
Knowing I won't be alone.

When the sun starts setting
And the minutes creep slowly by
It will be worth the time
To see your face again.

As all the things we shared
Pass through the mirrors of my mind.
Seems like it's been forever
Since I looked into your eyes.
So welcome back.
I really missed you.

#361 August 15, 1973. Another visiting angel returns home.

Angels

Angels fly across my room
To guard me in the night
Watching over my sleeping soul. Making sure everything is right.

They send out vibrations
I'd pick up in my sleep
Which gives me that feeling
Of happiness I need.

So shine down on me, angel
Let me ride on your
Golden wings and
Lift me above all my sorrow.

Show me
What happiness brings.
Little angels keep me company,
As they done throughout the years.

Been by my side of times in joy.
Wept with me in times of tears.

#362 August 16, 1973. When angels call, you need to answer the door, because they don't stay long.
Artwork of Archangel Raphael, 1974.

Traveling Lady

She is a traveling lady
Who sparkles in the night
And glistens in the sunset
With the stars by her side.

She took to the highway in search of a dream.
With no strings to bind her or to find a reason for being.

Someone stole your heart away.
And just like so many others.
None of them were bound to stay.

So where is your raincoat
Can't you see it's going to storm?
Before the tears get in your eyes
You better find another home.
So where will you go now that it's time to leave?
Will you move on to another one and leave his soul in the street?

Never love a traveling lady.
She'll steal your heart away.
Words of promises and fantasies.
A traveling lady will never stay.

#365 August 28, 1973. She liked the open road, but couldn't find her home.
Art portrait of Keli, February 1973.

Life's Little Games

She was just mixed up
And thought she had her world together.
When she sat down to look around,
Seems she's been lost forever.

She's looking for an answer to fill her empty head.
And with all of her questions
She wishes she were somewhere else instead.

She took a needle to her soul
To wash all her troubles away.

Don't bother to wait or question if tomorrow's another day.
She used shine so bright and light up everyone's dreams.
Now she lives in a nightmare.
Seems like rain is all it brings.

#370 September 17, 1973. A veiled warning to all lost fancy dancers passing by.

Shapeless Clouds

The morning paper says rain today.
But there's not a cloud in the sky.
The sun is shining brightly
And reflecting in my eyes.

Sent her away on a rainy day
Looking for small break in the clouds.
And I ask myself on a cloudy day.
Should I wrap my life in a shroud.

Rainbows seem to glitter
Only after a storm.
And shapeless clouds seem
To take another form.

Should I put on a rain coat
And bundle up my frozen ears.
Too many storms caught me unaware
That raindrops are only tears.

#378 September 21, 1973. There once was a time when I didn't fear the rain.

Raindrops in a Storm

We are but raindrops in a storm
Changing like the seasons, never lasting
We are plentiful like the moving clouds
Passing over civilizations

We are fruitful as the green grass
Covering over the mountainside
Wasteful as the sun's cosmic rays
Pounding against a barren desert floor

We are conditioned like the seasons
Changing in a continuous cycle
We rise and fall like moisture
Frozen in the winters rain

We drop like leaves from a tree
And sprout like little seedlings
We are a beginning
We are an end.

Robert Edward Jackson
#408
Jan. 2, 1974

#408 January 2, 1974. Copy of original.

We are but raindrops in a storm
Changing like the seasons, never lasting
We are plentiful like moving clouds
Passing over civilizations

We are fruitful as the green grass
Covering over the mountainside
Wasteful as the sun's cosmic rays
Pounding against a barren desert floor

We are conditioned like the seasons
Changing in a continuous cycle
We rise and fall like moisture
Frozen in the winter's rain

We drop like leaves from a tree
And sprout like little seedlings
We are a beginning
We are an end.

#408 January 2, 1974. Trying to be optimistic even during a rainstorm.

New Year's Eve

I had her under my finger but I let her go.
Without telling where. Without her even knowing.

I looked into her eyes, staring into space, into mine
We traveled the universe. I was floating. She was flying.

And she uncovered a dream
And told her story.
Deep within
She was New Year's Eve
And I was her guide.
Taking her through reality
By journeying through her eyes.

So, New Year's Eve,
You're gone and so go your memories
Of what we shared deep inside
Upon awakening, we didn't see.

#409 January 2nd, 1974. To Cookie, from Texas. Happy New Year's Eve.

Choo-Choo's

I walked around these wooden floors before.
I danced a tune around these tables.
I drank the wine and guzzled the beer.
I stumbled home when I was able.

And I called out for another beer.
It used to rob my guts away.
When I was stoned, they carried me home
To rest up for another day.

With a bottle of beer and cigarettes,
I was the man of the thousand dances.
Wasting my time, drinking cheap wine.
Watching my life dreaming fancy.

Jukebox music brings fond memories
Of those wooden floors and raunchy tables.
And the ladies in waiting,
Wearing cheap perfume,
They'll still dazzle the sober away.
Some have passed on. Some are gone
To other towns with other names.
And this was home for those few
Who danced every night at Choo-Choo's.

#411 January 7, 1974. Choo-Choo's was home to many fancy dancers and their lovers on 4th Avenue.
Clip art of two drunken dancers.

My Long Road

Years pass by and so do many more people with their own Traveling Shows.

Traveler

Five years I've followed the road
    To whichever way it would lead me.
        Settled down into a town for awhile
Before making another journey.

The streets were sprinkled with passersby's

Strolling along a lonely avenue of cold.

Their faces begging for dimes.

Digging their graves, paying their dues.

No one could see what they are doing.

For it's shoved to the back of our heads.

Dying junkies rotting by the needle.

Living ones wishing they were dead.

The streets are home to lonely travelers

Finding a place to rest their bones.

A smoke one can spare or even some change.

No belongings to own, the world is their home.

The jukebox music in a honky café.

Too many smokes fog my mind.

A cup of coffee chilling away.

Bottomless cups filled for a dime.

Late night hours, another town to travel.

Seems like only yesterday I've been gone.

People on the road tell me

It's time to settle down for a while.

Maybe it's time to unravel

A song of better days with happier smiles.

Doesn't it matter where the time has gone

With some many more roads to travel?

#412 January 6, 1974. It's been 5 years since I started writing poems. We are all travelers.
Artwork of wooden traveler.

Story lines

*G*uess it's time to turn another page.

For all the writing has been done.

All the actors have left the stage.

It's time for the curtain to come down.

And I write my final lines to an empty theater

That watched me with blind eyes,

And listened with silent ears.

Late night hours writing scenes.

But the tragedy that seems to reply
Circles of tears that seemed to weave
Cobwebs for another day.

The critics can't seem to understand
Why the story has to be so sad.
Seems like every episode is damned
Until a hero is finally dead.

Story lines written to please
An audience that plants the seed.

#420 January 30, 1974. We are also all producers of our own Traveling Show.
Clip art of an empty theatre.

Replacement

As I stare at the walls that once were my life,
Treading the waters that once made my home,
I walked along the avenues of my memories
And wrote lines to a world I once had known.

So hard to leave when you're so close behind
All of the sweet dreams you once had tasted.
So hard to see when you're almost gone blind
Into believing all your dreams have gone wasted.

And will I write my last poem to a dead world
That fills a void of stone cold faces?
With all of the lines I've left behind,
Will silence be its replacement?

#424 February 4, 1974. Lost in limbo. The angels are off to other realms.

Kaleidoscope

*A*nd seasons passed round against
A kaleidoscope of games.
Each moment another colour
With different meanings, they're still the same.

A couple of raindrops have fallen.
A tint of a rainbow is seen.
Making a kaleidoscope of colours.
Each one from another dream.

Too many reasons to waste away.
Yet more than enough to want to.
Kaleidoscope of forgotten things
Replaying songs someone once knew.

A little bit of sunshine
Upon a cloudy day.
Kaleidoscopes turning
Hopes for a brand new way.

#425 February 4th 1974. A constant changing of the seasons. I wait for more adventures and colors.

Sundown

#434 May 1, 1974. Age 20. Dedicated to Keli, Micky, Debbie and Beth. I sat and watched the sun set.

She followed like the seasons, constantly changing
Into dreams she once hoped to have been
That never were or ever will be
More than a fantasy's reality.

In the morning when she rises, she greets the sun
That follows the same path each day.
And, looking for a way to find home again
She washes her tears away in the rain.

Just like so many others
Caught in the web you weaved.
Sundown is coming, best beware,
If you want a sunrise near.

For what dreams she has, she finds a way
To follow the only world she knows.
Better wake up before it's too late.
'Cause the sundown may be close at hand.

#434 May 1, 1974. Predicting a dim future for perpetual travelers.

Rainbows

Rainbows

And how you change like the seasons
Into a world that's constantly new,
From part of the dreams you left behind
Of all the flowers that never grew.

Remember all the Welcome Backs
And how your wilted flowers faded,
With all the lines of comfort and love
That all the other times were made.

And, rainbow shows a slice
Of all the faded photographs,
That make up the memories
Of a child ~~beginning~~ growing up
innocent dreams

Robert Edward Zucker

Dedicated to
Terri Montgomery
July 3, 1974

#443 Original handwritten copy.

90

*A*nd how you change like the seasons
Into a world that's constantly new.
From part of the dreams you left behind
Of all the flowers that never grew.

Remember all the Welcome Backs,
And how wilted flowers faded.
With all the lines of comfort and love
That all the other times were made.

Each rainbow shows a slice
Of all the faded photographs
That make up the memories
Of innocent dreams growing up.

#443 June 26, 1974. Dedicated to Tami (Keli) on her welcome back, again.
Photo of Keli and Bob, 1973.

Player in a band

*C*onnie was a dancer,
And she played in a band.
She floated in my dreams
And stole away my heart.

She came from the City,
Across the Golden Gate.
She traveled the countryside
Down from Half Moon Bay.

Jeanette was a singer
From the Strip in LA.
And she traveled each night
To south of the Bay.

Nickels and dimes used to be their friends.
But they lost the pleasure that brought death instead.

So travel, little ladies.
You've come along way
Lost all you ever known.
And dug yourself a grave.

#426 February 7, 1974. Some never learned how hard the road feels until they fall.

Circus

*H*ere I am, once again,
A cup of coffee in my hand.

Waitress looking over my shoulder
Waiting for me to order.

And summer time comes around again.
Another new story to tell.

But already it's chapter five.
And a year has barely passed by.

It's beginning once again.

The wheel travels around in circles.
And as it weaves, a web it leaves
That keeps me in this circus.

#438 June 5, 1974. There is never enough time to slow down when angels keep coming back again.

To All Back Home

*S*eems like the world is changing
    Each time I go back home.
    Somehow it seems so strange
In this world I had never known.

Am I growing, rearranging?
Building my life into something new.
And has the past gone and faded
In the things that I never knew?

Was it the smoke that got in my eyes
Which let me see what I was afraid?
Of knowing what would be true
That memories are kept and not made.

Sorry that I must say goodbye.
Sorry to say that I'm leaving.
But the road was long and weary
And it's time to stop believing.

People change and so does time.
And I guess the change was me.
Guess it was wrong to come back home
But I had to look to see.

And the world spins around again.

And life is a very long road.

But you know where a smile comes

It is from one long ago.

Maybe I'll wait for a while

Till the road again calls my name.

And I'll make it all in style

Instead of playing little games.

Guess the road was too long to travel.

#444 August 15, 1974. Revisiting places of younger days- never the same again. Keli taught me that.
A grainy photo of Keli standing on a small town road back at her home still etched on my mind.

Traveling Future Roads

The following poems focus back on my own travels on life's dusty roads.

Steering my own Ship of Fools off the coast of California, early-1980s.

Where do dreams go

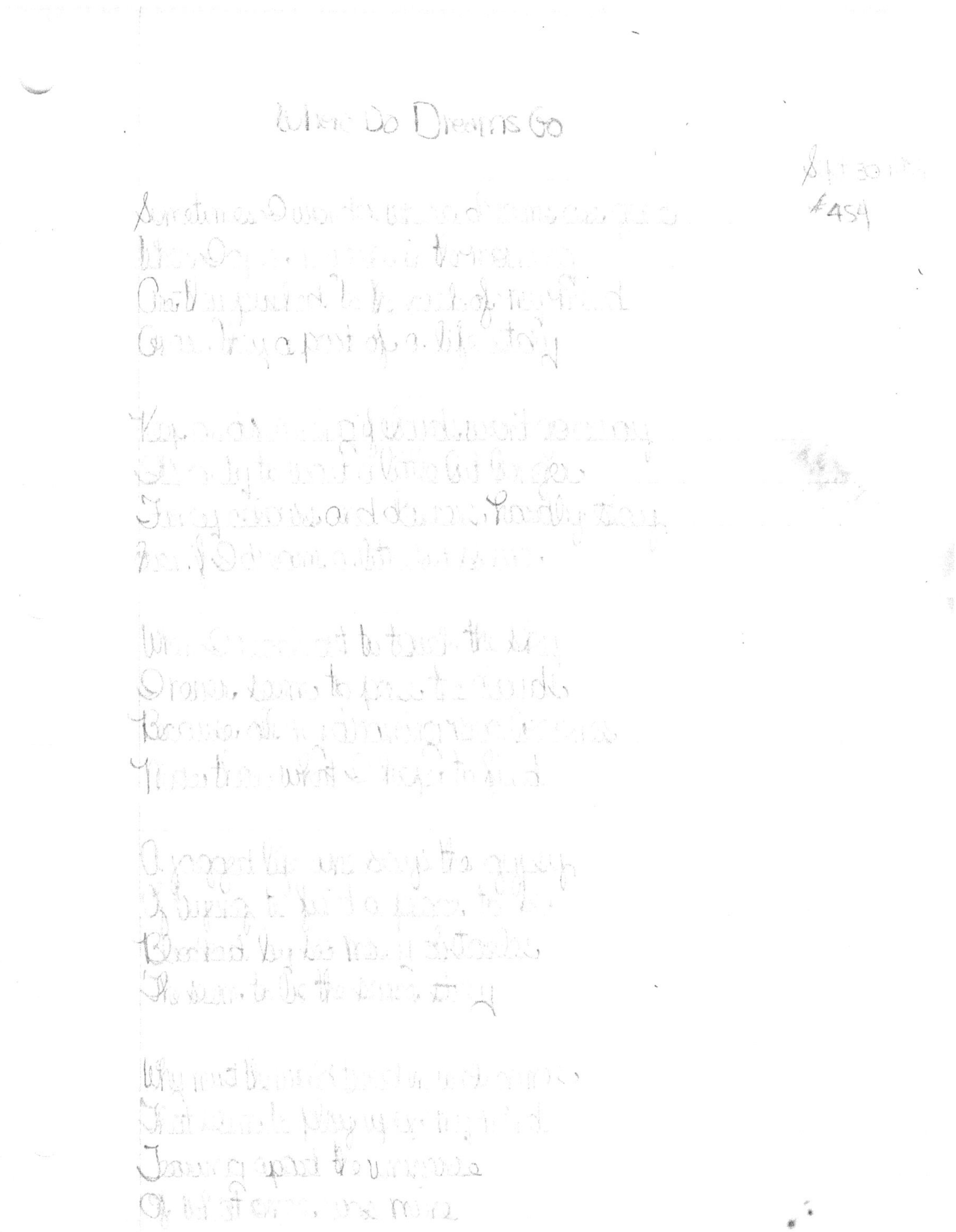

*S*ometimes I wonder where dreams are gone
When I open my eyes in the morning.
Are they pushed to the back of my mind,
Or are they a part of a life story.

Keep on dreaming if clouds won't go away.
It's only to wait a little bit longer.
Fancy colours and dancers hardly stay
Even if I dream a little bit slower.

When I reach out and touch the sky,
I never seem to pass the clouds.
Because all my dreaming never becomes
More than what I hope to find.

A jagged life line, says the gypsy
Of trying to find a place to be.
Blocked by so many obstacles
That seems to be the same story.

Why must the world travel in circle games
That seem to play upon my mind.
Tearing apart the universe
Of what once was mine.

#454 September 30, 1974. After awakening, the dream quickly disappears- almost like the passerby's.

Old Man

O ld man,
Where do you wander?
Past all the years you have known.

Sweet dreams
That keep on growing.

Forgotten ones
Growing old.

Old man, are you still counting the
days that quickly slipped by.

And are they only reminders of the
limits of your time?

Shaded by memories that passed
your weakening eyes.

After so many years of reaching
have you finally touched the sky?

#453 September 16, 1974. I still keep
reaching somewhere, too – 40 years later.
"Ancient of Days" Artwork drawn in 1978.

Dream

I *dreamed that I was at a party*
With an ex-old friend of mind.
The lights were low, but music high.
So much had changed our lives.

We talked about the heavens and
How much fun it was getting there.
And, all of the hills
We tried to climb,
All forgotten dreams
We shared.

A field of roses in the valley
Are coming to take me home.
And, it's the flowers I've been picking
Of the dreams that have grown too old.
She hung her head low
She said she was ashamed.
She touched my soul
I guess I did the same.

Dream about your new home.

And, the tenderness you brought me.
Sweet songs you have sung.
I guess it wasn't a dream.

#456 October 4, 1974. Sometimes, dreams do become real. But, most often, they fade away.
Artwork of Kathy asleep by the fireside, 1975.

A long time, hello - goodbye

Thursday, she called on the telephone.
"It's been a long time,
And I'm feeling down.
Just need someone to talk to.
Thinking of coming back home."

"The weather's real cold.
And it's been snowing around.
Sure would like to feel the sun.
What it have you been up to?"

"Yes, I changed my style.
Very few bars and cigarettes.
Going back to work real soon.
Just doesn't seem like me."

"Changing, yes, rearranging.
Guess it's just about time.
And I haven't forgotten you.
How can you forget a piece of your life?"

Have you climbed to the clouds, I wondered?
Did they cause you the trip and fall?
Are you searching for salvation
In what you left long ago?

"Sure would like to see you. Been a hell of a long time.
Recovering from a casualty
We once both had shared."

"Got your letter Wednesday.
Really sorry to hear.
Still feel the same as always.
March is almost near."

Her last words were "I love you."
I said the same.
Sat down to spin my head around.
Was it just another game?

She once traveled over the heavens
Glistening like a sunrise.
She touched my soul and sparkled
When I looked deep into her eyes.

Pages of lines and pictures
Are all that's left behind
Of dreams that seemed to crumble
With hardly a goodbye.

Just mountains and royal chariots
Only walls to block my view.
But hidden webs of mystery
That I thought I once knew.

Which way the wind blows

Guess I'll follow there.

Got some time to wander around

Til I find another web to share.

But I couldn't understand the rainbows

Until it was just too late.

Maybe another chance I'll have

To change the story my way.

#465 December 23rd 1974. The eve of Christmas Eve and the phone rings, again. Keli says hi.
Artwork of desert and mountains near Reddington Pass, mid-1970s.

Spinning circles

*S*pinning circles inside a circle game.
Watch the children cross the road.
Look for the sun on the cloudy day.

Spinning circles
ever more.

Flowers that grow in winter,
But, don't bloom til spring.
Keeps seasons spinning
In circles.
Keeps the wind blowing
Through the trees.

Isn't it time to touch the ground.
Circles keep spinning constantly.
Sweet dreams that only step aside
Of the spinning circles of reality.

#466 December 28, 1974. The cycle keeps spinning and I'm getting dizzy.
Clip art of spinning circles.

Eve of New Years Eve

*C*offee grounds and I'm spinning around.
Writing lines for a dime.
Though it won't snow,
It's been very cold.
So many clouds on my mind.

The waitress smiles, says it's been awhile
Since she's seen my face around.
Nothing is changed, three years the same
To be picked up when I'm feeling down.

The long nights of beer and cigarettes
That only fog my mind.
Faded dreams into memories
Lets me slip off for awhile.

The eve of New Year's Eve.
Round three times the season.
I'm already home, on my own.
Isn't that enough of reason?

Reflecting, always reflecting
Into a bottomless cup for a dime.
Changing, only rearranging
All words put into lines.

Spin a vicious circle.

Just new flavors to the words.
The waitress fills my coffee
From a request I never made.

Look at the dreams shine in my cup
Bringing me right back to the ground.
Traveling lady, are you so crazy
Don't know when you'll come around.

The eve of New Year's Eve.
Round three times the season.
Three cups I've downed
Just one more around
To keep my head from spinning.

#470 December 30th 1974. Waiting and wondering if she'll be back a fourth time this year.

Tues. December 31, 1974
1:20 AM

472

THOUGHTS

Just ramblings through my mind
in the words of a poem
lines that tell stories
of the world in changes
that fade into the pages of time
in the words of a poem.

Don't really know why I'm doing it this way. Maybe a few words say
more than a few pages of ramblings. Yet, they only hold a meaning
for me, if nothing else.

Guess it was the music I heard that got me to change my style.

Changing...maybe just rearranging.

I'm only a poem
A poem I'm meant to be
And just like a poem
I'm the story of me.

—Maybe someone will understand.

#472 December 31st 1974. Original handwritten copy. I'm trapped inside a poem.

Thoughts

*J*ust ramblings through my mind
In the words of the poem.
Lines that tell stories
Of the world in changes
That fade into the pages of time
Into the words of the poem.

Don't really know why I'm doing it this way.
Maybe a few words say,
More than a few pages of ramblings.
Yet only they hold a meaning
For me, if nothing else.

Guess it was the music I heard
That got me to change my style.
Changing, maybe just rearranging.

I'm only a poem.
A poem I'm meant to be.
And just like a poem.
I'm the story of me.

#472 December 31st 1974, age 20. Goodbye 1974. Maybe someone will understand.

Picture Show

Crowds and the wind blows.
Waitresses running around.
She stops long enough to smile,
Making a cold night into a warm one.

People in worn overcoats.
A little of the seasons cheer.
The hurried look on their faces
Of bringing in another year.

One more time to be, again,
Another hopeless wanderer.
But if I reach the ground
Instead of spinning around
I'll know just where I've been.

It used to be these were the seasons
Which keep changing before my eyes.
Shared three times round
In my coffee grounds.
Shared in the middle of the night.

Revolving doors keep on turning
Like a wheel with no destiny.
Frightened away, with nothing to say
What more is there to lose?

A couple of chances to change the world.
Maybe only icebergs in my mind.
Sweet dreams, she said, on the day she left.
After, I said, another goodbye.

Only words for those
Who think they listen
But only answer with the stare.

Just more thoughts
Which come like picture shows
Just a couple of lines to share.

#473 January 1st 1975. Starting a new year while recovering from the last one.

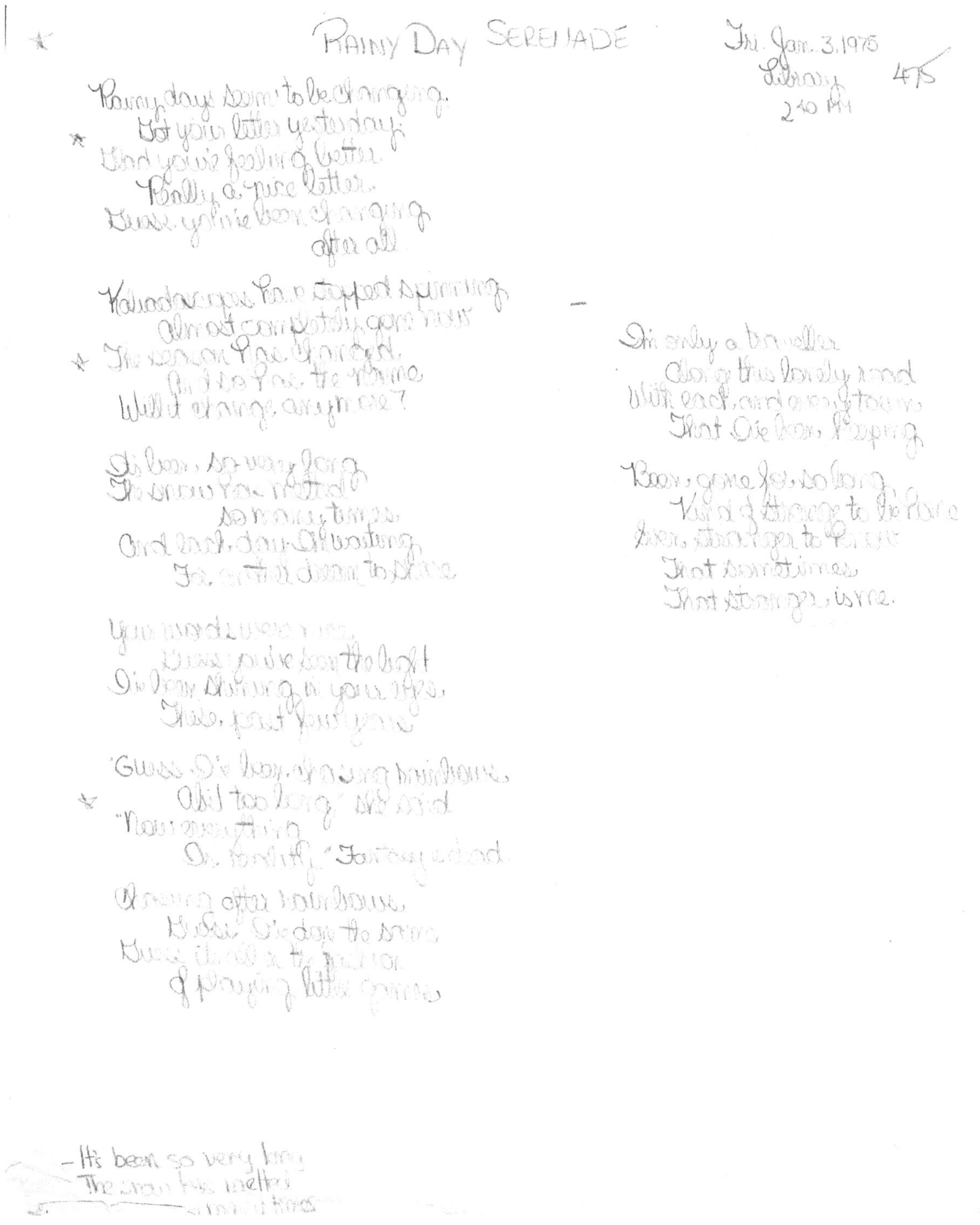

RAINY DAY SERENADE

Fri. Jan. 3, 1975
Library
2:40 PM
475

Rainy days seem to be changing.
Got your letter yesterday;
Glad you're feeling better.
Really a nice letter.
Guess you've been changing
after all

Kaleidoscopes have stopped spinning
Almost completely gone now
The season has changed.
[illegible] the rhyme
Will it change anymore?

It's been so very long
The snow has melted
so many times
And each day [illegible] waiting
For another dream to share

Your words were [illegible]
Guess you've seen the light
I've been shining in your life.
These past few years

"Guess I've been chasing rainbows
A bit too long," she said
"Now everything
Is [illegible] "Fantasy is dead.

Chasing after rainbows,
Guess I've done the same
Guess it's all in the [illegible]
of playing little games

I'm only a traveller
Along this lonely road
With each and every town
That I've been keeping

Been gone for so long
Kind of strange to be home
Even stranger to know
That sometimes
That stranger is me.

-It's been so very long
The snow has melted
so many times

#475 January 3, 1975. Original handwritten copy. It's been so long. The snow has melted..

Rainy Day Serenade

Rainy days seem to be changing.
Got your letter yesterday.
Glad you're feeling better.
Guess you been changing after all.

Kaleidoscopes have stopped spinning.
Almost completely gone now.
The seasons have changed
And so has your name.
Will it change any more?

"Guess I been chasing rainbows
A bit too long," she said.
Now, everything that is reality.
Fantasy is dead.

I'm only a traveler
Along this lonely road.
With each and every town
That I've been keeping.
Been gone for so long.
Kind of strange to be home.
Even stranger to know
That sometimes
That stranger is me.

#475 January 3, 1975, age 20. She's been chasing rainbows in the rain and she's on the road home.

Raindrops in the morning

ain dripping off the rooftops.
Past mid morning, I arise.
No way to greet the New Year,
Except with sleep in my eyes.

Early morning coffee.
The clocks says almost ten.
She smiles, the time is getting late.

Rain drops in the morning.
Not really a feeling I have.
But it seems the clouds are still here.
Why must they have to hurry back?

What's the reaction of a side street show?
Sometimes it makes me wonder.
Who was afraid, the people or me?
That someone is going to blunder?
Maybe a new horizon.
Some of the plants arise.
Just waiting for the sunshine
To glide past my eyes.

A couple of old friends came by to spread some cheer.
Sort of saying goodbye to the old, and bring in a new year.

#474 January 1st 1975. Where is this year going to take me this time?

Omens

*S*ing a simple song to carry you away,
Past all the clouds to the heavens.
Words written only to convey

Thoughts which reach out like omens.

Champagne and beer on Saturday eve.
A corner street bar that sells time.
A step in the past of only memories,
Brought to life in a couple of lines.
Omens that tell of rainbows to follow
That seemed to bring you back home.

Laughter in the rain on the other side
Of a rainbow with a pot of gold.
Every other line she seems to say
Things that were hard to say before.
In between the words that she wrote
Seem to be in search of new stars.
New dreams this season with lots of time

To sit back to watch this picture show.
If I reach really high enough
Will it be time to stop traveling along this dusty road?

#477 January 5th 1975. I should have read the road signs in her letters much more closely.
Artwork of woman waiting with a unicorn, circa 1975.

Chasing Rainbows

Sat Jan. 5 1975
Library
3:20 PM   416

Have I been chasing rainbows,
            all this time
In rainbows eyes of colours
And dreams I tried soon to
            disappear
Into the thoughts of another.

Your face brought the sunshine
            on a cloudy day
Changing like seasons
            on a winter's day

Will the smile be the same
On a little bit brighter for me.
Waiting, waiting farther, waiting
To break what used to be.

Sunrise has lost the sunshine
That used to light the sky
Guess I've been chasing rainbows
That flash before my eyes.

-Guess I've been chasing rainbows

#478 January 5, 1975. Original handwritten copy.

Chasing rainbows

H*ave I been chasing rainbows*
A bit too long
In kaleidoscopes of colours
And dreams I held seem to disappear.

Keli has brought the sunshine on a cloudy day
Changing like seasons on a winter's day.

Will the smile be the same,
Or a bit brighter for me?
Waiting seems forever waiting
To know what will be.

Sunrise has lost the sunshine
That used to light the sky.
Guess I've been chasing rainbows
That flashed before my eyes.

#478 January 5, 1975. Guess I've been chasing too many rainbows.

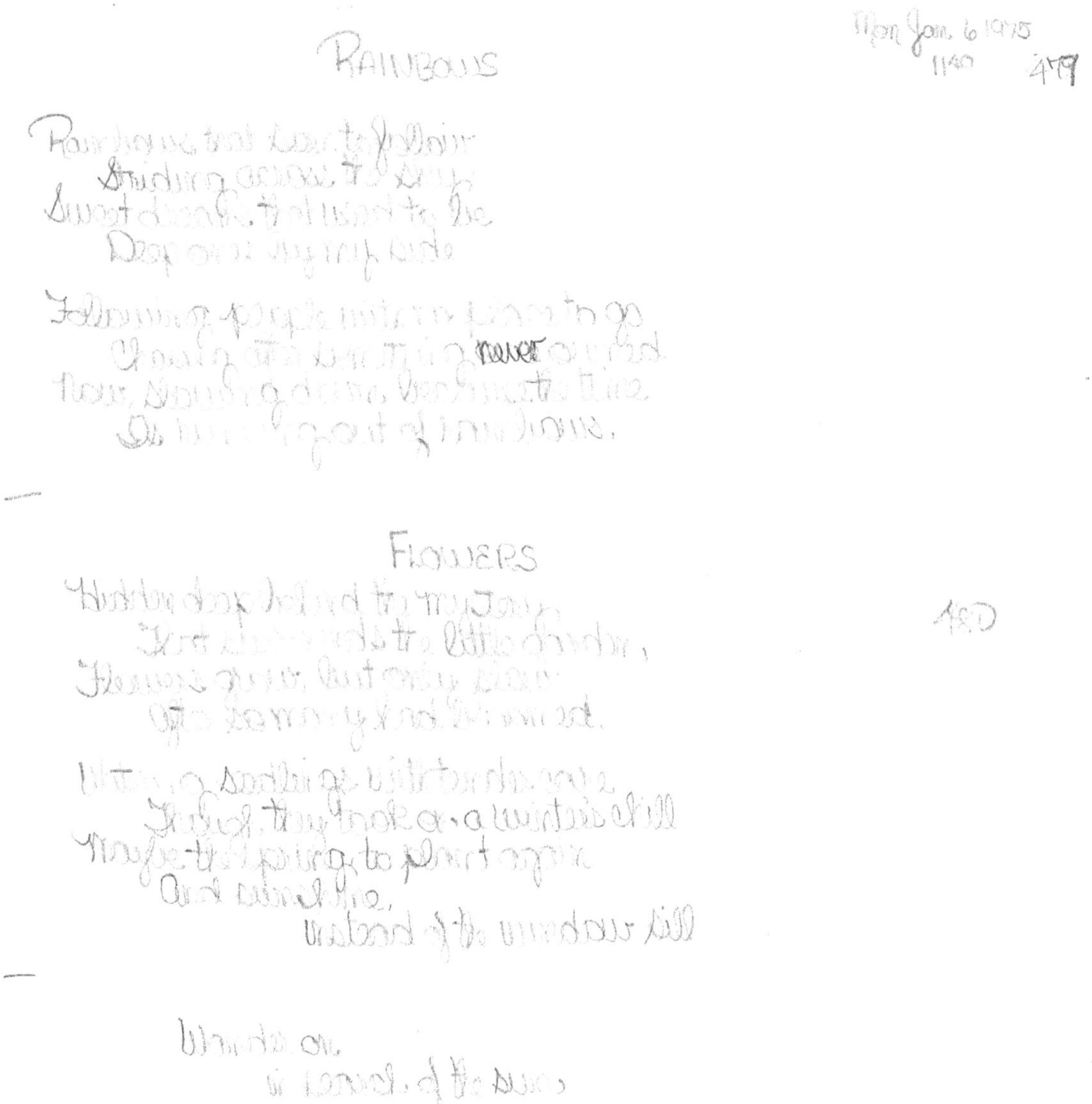
Mon Jan. 6 1975
479
RAINBOWS
FLOWERS
480

#479-480 January 6, 1975. Original copy.

Rainbows and flowers

R ainbows that seem to follow
Striding across the sky
Sweet dreams that used to be
Deep ones by my side.

Following people with no place to go
Chasing after something never owned.
Now, slowing down because the time
Is running out of rainbows.

F lowers
Hidden deep behind the mystery
That surrounds the little garden.
Flowers grow, but only slow
After so many had bloomed.

Watering seedlings with tender care,
Though, they took on a winter's chill.
Maybe the spring to plant again.
And sunshine
Instead of the window sill.

Wander on in search of the sun.

#479-480 January 6, 1975. Caught myself chasing rainbows and collecting flowers. Lost track of time.

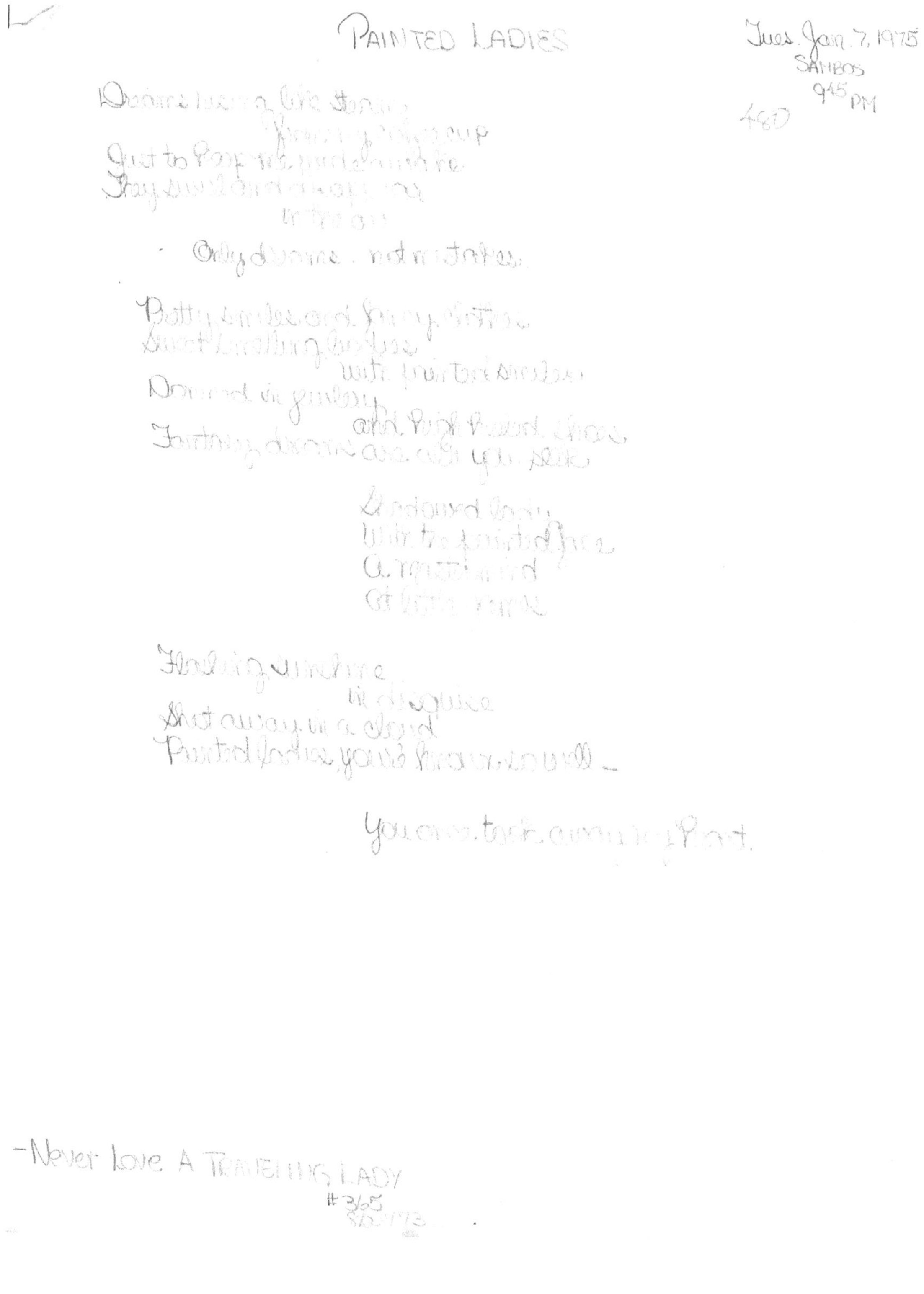
PAINTED LADIES
Tues. Jan. 7, 1975
SAMBOS
480
-Never love A TRAVELING LADY
#365

#480 January 7, 1975. Original copy.

Painted Ladies

D reams rising like steam
From my coffee cup.
Just to keep me wide awake,
They swirl and disappear in the air.
Only dreams...not mistakes.

Pretty smiles and fancy clothes.
Sweet smelling bodies with painted smiles.
Donned in jewelry and high heeled shoes.
Fantasy dreams are all you seek.

Shadowed lady
With the painted face
A mastermind
At playing games.

Flashing sunshine in disguise.
Shot away in a cloud
Painted ladies, you're known so well.

You once took away my heart.

#480 January 7, 1975. Never love a traveling lady.

IN BETWEEN LINES

10∞ PM
477

Picking up my pencil
            to write
The words to another poem
My mind runs a little
            and the words seem to fade
Out into the night
            Carried on the wind

Tattered jeans and a leather coat
Rings on my fingers
                that tell of times
Poems with no meaning
                but only to me
So my life written in between lines

Dames on my mind
            in which matter
That are only reflected in a poem
All of the things that come to be me
        Are found in between lines...

A system that's formed
            from, image words
I write to believe my hopes
But to grow with a little time
        just writing
                thinking
        I what I have said

−I'm Only A Poem

#484 January 7, 1975. Original copy.

In Between Lines

P icking up my pencil to write
The words to another poem
My mind draws a blank.
And the words seem to fade
Out into the night
And into the cold.

Tattered jeans and leather coat
Rings of my fingers that tell of times
Poems with my no meaning but only to me
Is my life written in between lines.

Games on my mind and silhouettes
That are only shaded by a pen
Of all of things that seem to be me
Are found in between lines.

A system that's formed
From meager words
I write to relieve my head.
Out to form with a little time
Just waiting,
Thinking
Of what I have said.

#477 January 6, 1975. I'm only a poem. Thus, the story is in-between the lines.

Sweet dreamer

C aught in the middle
Of a revolving door
Shared secrets of the universe
Undecided as before.

What's the secret locked inside
Just biding my time.
Really quite hard to decide
When the words need to rhyme.

Passing each day in a round about way.
Hoping for the time to slide by.

Another word, I pray to come my way.
Am I just running around in the night?

Go on sweet dreamer, dream
With lots of thoughts on your mind.
Some have come, and some of gone
And others will stay in time.

So many things will be different now.
Soon, I may hear myself say.
But which ones will be the reality.
Right now, I just can't say.

#482 January 7, 1975. Too many roads to travel in the night. Beth had so many sweet dreams.

Another welcome back

I watched you chase after rainbows
In search of the sun
That seemed so far away.

And like an angel without wings
Trying to touch the sky,
You tripped and fell instead.

Yet, chasing through your mind you seem
To find all the dreams that got away.
Spinning around in circles to reach
The ground, you watch the rainbows fade.

And, everything is reality when you're chasing after rainbows.
And, dreams are only fantasies that cause reflections and makes them glow.

Sometimes you seem almost a million miles away.
When will you ever reach those stars?
As you go searching in what you can find inside,
Look beyond the shadows in your eyes
It's been a long time...

Another welcome back to another crazy game.
But, if you have the strength and all the faith
You're only growing just to change.

#485 January 8, 1975. When you tripped and fell, there I was. A traveling lady comes around again.
Clip art of a child stumbling in a hole.

What did I do this Christmas vacation

I went chasing after rainbows when I couldn't find the sun.

Sat down to spin around only to fog my mind.

Rock and roll circle games. Loud music, women and beer.

Dentist chairs and Novocaine.

Writing poems and sitting here.

Made new friends and partied.

Sobering over some coffee.

Sleeping late and dreaming sleep.

Just trying to pass some time.

#487 January 8, 1975. The holiday was more than just celebration.
Taking a ride on the dragon Artwork, 1973.

126

Another Day

*A*nother day passing by.
Trees rustling in the wind.
Another winter day.

Walking down a Sunday street.
Stopped and asked for change.
Little lady selling jewelry.
Shared a few words for a while.

All the words were put away.
Packaged for tomorrow.
What will they say and answer.
Have I wasted my time?

Where are you from?
Michigan. It's too cold.
Been here long?
A few days or so...

#492 January 12th 1975. Meeting another passerby.

Dreams in her pocket

She looked out over the highway
For a car or for a dream.
Not able to understand
Just what her world is doing.

Backpack and cigarettes,
Sometimes, a girl's only friend.
When she follows fancy daydreams
That chase around with no end.

And I thought of you on the highway,
All alone in the cold.
And I'm worried what was happening,
Inside you're confusing world.

The lady was a traveler
Who loved the open road.
She carried her dreams in her pocket
She thought was filled with gold.

#493 January 12th 1975. There was a common thread among the travelers- the lure of an open road.

Roses and carnations

Her eyes are worn.
She holds her cup of coffee smelling dreams.
And her grey hair curls down her face.
Reflections that rise like steam.

The years have worn your face.
Faded by endless time.
Counting the days ticking away.
Dreaming in nursery rhymes.

Bitter and sorry for all the years
The bottle hugged your side.
The only pleasure of fancy dreams
That passed before your eyes.

Roses and carnations,
Are we all like you?
Only younger and not so trapped
In what we see in you.

Bundled for the evening
That still brings on a chill.
Nursing the wounds of the past
A bit of coffee spills.

#494 January 12th 1975. To the older lady sitting alone in Sambo's Restaurant.

Mon. Jan. 13, 1975
8 PM   495

Traveling Man

I closed the front door and slipped outside.
    Midmorning.
The wind still kind of growing.
The leaves I'm so glad. O
    I wonder.

Believing in things that amaze us.
    But only bad actors
By the parking garage and apostrophe
    Of colors that were only christine.

        Head up the [illegible] eyes of them
        And all the [illegible]
            And the quick grime.
                there's just the same
        As a [illegible]

Can you tell me which way you're going?
I that pardon your back turning
            can lighten your load
too long, have you been [illegible]
            Are you on the right road.

He lifted his eyes, lined with care,
            and said
        Simply a traveling man...

#495 January 13, 1975. Original copy.

Traveling Man

I closed the front door and stepped outside.
Midmorning.
The wind stopped blowing.
The flowers have died. It's winter.

Believing in things that never were,
But only lead astray
By the passing hours and spectrums
Of colours that were only dreams.

Here's to the flowing cups of beers
And all the cheap talk it buys.
And the circle games
They're just the same
As a pack of two-bit lies.

Can you tell me which way you're going?
Is that pack on your back heavy?
Can I lighten your load?
How long have you been traveling?
Are you on the right road?

He lifted his eyes lined with age, and said,
I'm only a traveling man.

#495 January 13, 1975. I'm only a traveling man. Through my eyes, I've carried her burdens.

Traveling

*L*ooking out over the highway and hoping for a ride.
  Clutching her pack and cigarettes
  Holding her dreams inside.

Traveled the road so many years.
Settling a town for a spell.
But not for long, she's up again
And spinning around.

Looking over the mountains that slice deep into the sky.
The sun is setting, cooling off, waiting for the stars to rise.

Just wandering alone
In search of a place
To call home.

Just traveling wherever you can
To find a place to call your own.
And people passed by your way
Sometimes with a smile.

Some stay, others fade away
Some even more than awhile.

#499 January 15, 1975. I'm not the only traveler through time.

A long time

H ello, she smiled,
But still so far away.
After so long
Things have changed.

But what could I say
Except, how are you?
It's been so long.
Tell me, what's new?

When I have nothing to say
Because so much has changed,
But still not sure what to do.
Don't want to play any games.
Where is the cloud that you hid in?
What made you come out again?

For fancy dancers are still dancing
Even after the music ends.

It's good to hear your voice again.
It's been quite a long time.
Yet, things have changed.
How can I explain if I have the time?

#500 January 17, 1975. Will it be another welcome back, again?

Clouds and Mountains

W*e talked on the phone last night*
For an hour and the sunset.
Spoke of what's on our minds
And all of things we've missed.

In a couple of weeks I'll see you again
To talk of all that's been done.
It seems you changed.
But that's only your name.
And even that has changed once before.

So many clouds and mountains.
So many bridges and walls.
But I guess I know you better
Than you know yourself at all.

You've been traveling on a rainbow.
Fell into your pot of gold.
And weave a new dream from an older story
In another one that's told.

#505 January 20th 1975. The rainbow peaks through the clouds. She's on the road again.

Wandering Daydreams

Wandering daydreams
Past wind blown trees.
Rustling leaves changing colours each season.

Pages on my mind tell of stories never ending
That seemed to fade with time.

And a dance the fancy dancer does
As she floats across the stage.
Pretty eyes and colorful clothes.
Hoping she will stay.

And all the other fancy dancers
Who once had made their way
Were just painted ladies and statuettes
That danced around each day.

When will the sun start shining
On broken hearted dreams?
Just waiting for the morning
To see what the next day brings.

#506 January 22nd 1975. Another season comes around, again. How long will it last this time?

Springtime freshness

*S*oft, spoken words from long ago,
Tomorrow's dreams and constant streams,
Make up this Traveling Show.

Am I a spinner in this constant game?
A seeker for a thrill?
Have I retired, after being so tired
Of spinning around in circles?

Reread all the written lines.
Collected thoughts and rhymes.
Just scribbled words, barely heard
But echoed many times.

Springtime freshness comes around again.
Time for another season.
Somehow it seems, whatever it means
It's the sunshine I've been needing.

#509 January 27, 1975. Getting tired of spinning around.

The Fancy Dancers

Fancy Dancers

and Thoughts on My Mind.

Wed. Jan. 29, 1975

512

G D C/G D C/G D C

Dreams

[illegible handwritten verse text, largely illegible]

#512 January 29, 1975. Original copy.

Fancy Dancers

*D*reams rising like steam
From my coffee cup
Just to keep me awake.
They swirl and disappear into the air.
Dreams...not mistakes.

Pretty smiles and fancy clothes
Sweet smelling bodies.
Warm painted smiles, jewelry,
And high heeled shoes
Dark stockings and long time blues.

And a dance
The fancy dancer does.
Floats across the stage.
Pretty eyes, colourful dress,
Fancy dancer, who's to be next?

And it's fancy dancers
And thoughts on my mind.
Just spinning my head around.
Chasing after flowers and rainbows.
Playing circle games
Along this traveling show.

#512 January 29, 1975. I only wish I was dreaming instead.

Fancy dancer in my hands, November 4, 1976 Artwork.

Fancy Dancing Dreams

S he traveled in the uncertainty of her ship made of gold.
Seeking to find serenity in what she lost long ago.

Guided by the wisdom she learned from her mistakes.

Looking for a kingdom,
Dreams she can replace.

Where is the serenity
You were seeking to find?

You turned to me for security
And a little piece of mind.

Fancy dancer,
Where is your home?
Across the aging sea.
Too young to know
When it's time to show
Fancy dancing dreams.

And it's fancy dancers and thoughts on my mind.
Just spinning my head around.
No words when they whisper quite softly.
They just keep on dancing so not to hear.

#511 January 27, 1975. Who's leading this ship of fools?
Clip art of the ship of fools.

Snow

*S*unshine morning
　Melting away the snow.
　Icicles dripping
Off winter's frozen trees.

It's sunshine this morning.
The snow's melting away.

The ground covered with
innocence.

Footprints in the show.
Just melting away.
Never again to be found.

The flames in the fireplace.
Dance a fancy tune.
My mind wanders with dreams
That seems to dance away.

#513 February 1, 1975. Thinking about those fancy dancers who have gone by.
Photo taken in 2008 on top of Mt. Lemmon after the fire.

Flowers, rainbows and sunshine

*T*hree dreams
Held out on a string.
Flowers, rainbows and sunshine.

With sunshine so close to home.
Rainbows close nearby.
And flowers keep on changing.
Can't understand why.

Flowers once bloomed.
Now, seem to fade away from a dream of long ago.
Kind of wish they would stay.

Rainbows still searching lost in the same storm.
Don't know where they're coming.
Don't know where they gone.

Now, sunshine shines brightly
Being obscured by the clouds.
Trying to be a bit brighter.
Lost, just waiting to be found.

And throughout all the seasons they keep me going around.
Just reaching out for some comfort.
Sure would rather touch the ground.

#518 February 19, 1975. Nothing lasts forever- just three seasons who keep coming around.

Minstrel Show

*I*n between the dreams the lines were written.
Only words just the same.

I feel like I'm in a Traveling Show.
Only dreams a spell away.
I just wanted to say something instead.

Sunday a.m. at one o'clock and here I sit in my dreams.
Saturday night just fading away
Into a triangle of rings.

Their faces - they seemed to linger
A little longer than their thoughts.
Their eyes - that are fogged and spinning
Fleeing, but never get caught.

Why spread the things which are only the reasons
Of thoughts just slipping away.
Looking to find a piece of mind
To fill my thoughts instead.

An empty stare to nowhere. So much on my mind.
A minstrel show with no place to go.
Only a space in time.

#522 March 2nd 1975. Their Traveling Shows make a stop in time. Three faces, three passing dreams.

Sweet dreams

S weet dreams and rainbows
Trying to reach the sun.
Reaching for serenity
In search of heaven.

Spring season with flowers to grow
Across the barren fields.
With the sun shining into your world
Sweet dreams can seem so real.

Summer breeze blowing in your hair
Sometimes carries you away.
And leads you to a stranger place
Sometimes leads you astray.

Autumn leaves changing colors
In each and every rainbow.
Confused by flashes before your eyes
With so many roads to follow.

Just take steps, one by one,
And open your eyes to the skies.
Open your heart to those who care.
Sweet dreams are so close by.

Winter's snow frozen by the cold.
Frozen deep in your heart and mind.

Waiting just to break the mold.
Sweet dreams you wish to find.

Deep in your heart, stored away
Is a light shining in your soul.
Flickering as a glorious flame
To brighten your beautiful world.

Just let your dreams dream on.
They're not that far behind.
Though the road seems dusty and long
Sweet dreams will come in time.

#524 March 5th 1975. For Beth at 19. Happy birthday. Seasons come around again. Sweet dreams.

Goodbye Tonight

Hours of words and you're gone away. Once again.
Sweet dreams and rainbows you failed to find.
Welcome back and goodbye.

Where are you headed
This time around?

It's hard to travel all alone
With so many places to go.

Each time you run
You think you're done.
Then, you start out all over again.

We have lost the words to explain
Of what we hide away.
We both kept on searching
For a rainbow to come
Yet, we run away in fear.
Aren't our paths the same?

Cool breeze in an open field.
My mind splits the night away.
Spinning around my head hung down.
Just wishing it would rain.

#525 March 7th 1975. Always in a rush to nowhere. She's gone once again.
Clip art of a woman leaving her lover.

Again

The band played a song on the radio
Now it's over, long gone.
Like the sweet song you heard before.
Sweet dreams, now, no more.

Like so many followers
Along this open road
To share some time and sit a spell
Before they head for home.

And it's fancy dancers
And thoughts on my mind
Spinning my head around.
Playing circle games
Along this Traveling Show.

Sweet dreams, flowers,
Champagne and rainbows,
And, a rendezvous.
Just waiting to settle home.

And an old friend said,
I don't understand.
I said, if you only knew.

#526 March 16, 1975. And again, they never stay long enough. Sweet dreams disappear in the night.

Myself

I *went looking for myself,*
And needing a reason.
I find in myself.
The hope I needed for dreams.

Where am I searching,
In whose backyard will I find,
The things I hope to share-
The dreams on my mind.

Guiding myself discretely
Trying to reach the sun
Lost in a cycle of confusion
My world, where else to run.

Reread all the thoughts before
In between lines forgotten
If one can see, I guess only me
Who else understands.

A musician, I sing my songs
To a room of smoke filled dreams.
A traveler, I travel on myself
As I find another home.

#527 March 16th 1975. Beth always had sweet dreams. Keli was always chasing rainbows. Artwork of cabin, Mt. Lemmon, 1974. Once in awhile, I need to travel.

Spring

S pring dreams keep on spinning.
It's such a long way from home.
Coffee steam, kind of windy,
Thoughts of you on my mind.

Open roads
That's the way it goes.
Kind of sad to see it end.

But spring's come 'round,
Find some clouds to share.
Find some dreams to make it shine.

All the circles spun so soon.
Didn't have time to settle down.
Now, the spring brings a new season.
What's the weather this time around?

Just a couple more things
That are lost in the cold.
Just too far away from my world.
But, maybe the spring
Will bring the sun to me.
Don't need the open road.

#530 March 21, 1975. 1 A.M. in Sambo's diner thinking about the spring, which is about to leave.

Beth

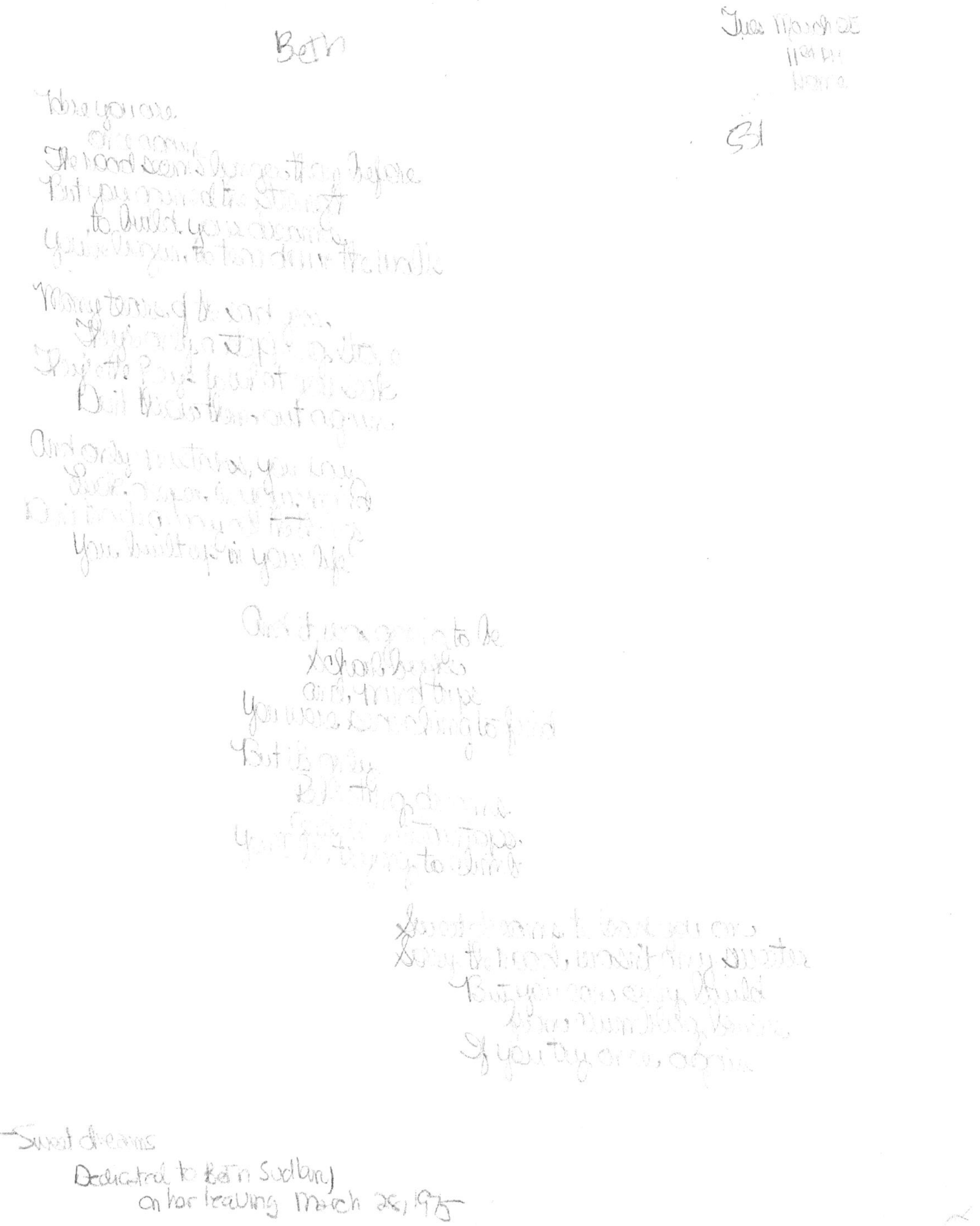

*H*ere you are
Once again.
The road seems longer than before.
But, you gained the strength to build your dreams.
You've begun to tears down the walls.

Many tears of the sad years.
They're only a stepping stone.
They're the keys to what you seek.
Don't throw them out again.

And it's only mistakes, you say.
Look deeper inside your mind.
Don't trade away all of things
You've built up in your life.

And it was going to be school books and mind trips
You were searching to find.
But it's only reflecting dreams and mountaintops
You'll be trying to climb.

Sweet dreams to lead you on.
Sorry the road wasn't any sweeter.
But, you can only build from crumbling bricks
If you try once again.

#531 March 25, 1975. Beth left this day with this poem. Sweet dreams. Beth passed away in August 2008.

Rainy Days and Wednesdays

The chill outside slowly seeps in.
The bus driver with coffee in hand.
The street lights just passing by.
All the dreams I had today.

Home seems so far away.
My home, farther still.
And a feeling in my soul
Telling me
I got my dreams
Now I need a home.

Rainy days and Wednesdays.
Sweet songs on the radio.
Feeling low, the weather's cold.
Bundle up for my Traveling Show.

#532 March 26, 1975. Am I happier without their fancy dancing dreams?

Another Goodbye

*H*ere I am,
Once again.
Time to turn another page.

For the writing's been done
From the words never said.
And sweet dreams are traveling
Relieving our heads.

No more cigarettes or worries.
No more tears that come in the night.
All the pages have been written.
No more thoughts to share tonight.

Now I understand
What you tried to say.
And what I left behind
Still deciding
On another day.

#534 March 30th 1975. The road is always open. There she goes, again.

Little Angels

O h, little angels.
Gone from home again.
Sorry the story seems so bad.

Never love a traveling lady,
I try so hard to say.
She'll just steal your heart away.
With sweet dreams and rainbows
So far away, and so hard to find.
A traveling lady never seems to stay.

Fancy dancers and circle games,
Just swimming my head around.
I reach for the sun
Barely touching the sky.
And, I always hit the ground.

#535 March 31, 1975. Keli's phone call. She's on her way back, again.

Passing time

P assing time
These days gone by.
Hoping to catch a dream.

Been spinning around
With new alibis.
Trying to figure out
What this all means.

Fancy dreamer
Here you go again
Trying to climb the walls.
Looking behind
The things you find
To get it together again.

Fading, like forgotten memories
In the endless and dreary of my soul.
Each turn just needlessly.
Each one another show.

#538 April 7th 1975. As I get ready to turn 21, I watch them still come and go.
Clip art of a woman holding an emptied hourglass among the ruins.

Where are they now?

Two bits and a head, she said.
She did all the dancing.
And, reaching for rainbows,
She wanted to touch the sky.

Sweet dreams confused by colours
Inside a kaleidoscope.

She sees the world through
Golden eyes,
Flowers and the sun.

Looking for rainbows.
She got lost in the clouds.

#541 April 13, 1975, age 21. Each has their own story fused into my Traveling Show.

Shattered Mirrors

*A*n opening to another poem,
One for another year.
Sweet roads to be conquering
Sweet dreams to be near.

Worn torn phrases worn with time,
Like turning another page.
All the things that once were mine
Are just circles spinning away.

All old friends say goodbye
When it's time to be leaving.
Making room for more sweet games.
Open space for breathing.

Beautiful visions pass me by.
What a long and lonely day.
The sun is just as far behind.
Shattered mirrors once again.

#542 April 14, 1975. Everyone has gone back home. My home is my own.

Drifter in Time

The pages were full of many words,
Lines that had been written before.
Poems, in thoughts
And words, in rhyme.
Words of a drifter in time.

She was the last of the poems
That passed like many more.
She was a drifter
Who drifted through my door.

And, home they made,
And stayed for awhile.
Sending and spending some bread.
And when the ride got too rough,
They packed up,
And drifted in time again.

#550 May 7, 1975. There wasn't much more than memories.

Smiling faces

*A*lthough smiling, lovely faces
Come to tap dance on my heart,
Sharing their sweet dreams
Spacing their sweet time
Fancy dancing into the night.

Backpacks and cigarettes welcomed for a stay.
Come tomorrow the highway takes them away.

Where are they headed?
Where have they gone?
Where are they coming from?

Security to be shared behind temporary dreams
Only to be stolen away by the night.
Looking inside daydreams and moonbeams
When wondering, it seems so right.

Stop myself from spinning around
Until I hit the ground, then wait.
Playing, and playing, those circle games.
Never time to settle down.
Only, when one has gone.
Another dances my way.

June 3, 1975. Years later, they still keep floating on by.

Bright lights and promises

She walked into the room
And closed the door.
"Another long day," she thought,
And took the scarf from her neck.

She closed the curtains,
Because the sun was shining
Too brightly into the room.
She turned on the music
That filled the walls
With tunes from long ago.

Bright lights and promises
Across the dusty road.
She looked into the mirror.
God, how time seems to grow.

She brushed her hair,
Her dreams in a comb.
And wishing it was yesterday,
Wishing she was home.

Her eyes filled with the same old tears.

Almost the same old story.

And, God, she knows,

She's changing it all.

Just another sunset dream.

She turned her face that's caked with makeup,

And her eyes that are covered with brow.

Growing older inside a mirror.

Yet, only younger against time.

Bright lights and promises,

Bound across the corner,

Hidden across the page.

She looked at the calendar,

Passing so many days.

She thought about the good ole times.

But, that was only in her name now.

She knew she had to change

To survive this world.

But, change is only her game now.

And she cries when things get lonely,

And turns pages so she can stay.

Wants to do some traveling.

Can't seem to make her way.

She went outside to feel the sun.

And walked along the unpaved road.

One that she never discovered.

One she never seen before.

She wasn't feeling as bad as it seems.

It wasn't as plastic as before.

The street was paved with golden dreams

That seemed to shine on more.

Bright lights and promises

To pave your own road.

She was only traveling

With her own Traveling Show.

#559 June 9, 1975. She had such bright lights and promises. But she ain't got no time.

Still traveling

S *tirring the ashes to another bowl of smoked filled rooms.*
No cigarettes.
No more time to spend.

Soon, a change.
Another picture show.
Which way do they come and go?

So much, to just set on down
All the dreams I've been keeping.
But so many stories change
And come around
To the shadows I've been seeking.

Unfulfilled promises
Made from customized dreams.
Each angel has to be floating
Above the starry heavens without wings.

And watch them drop
At the doorstep.
Welcome on home.
Never seen any better
Still traveling and searching on their own.

#588 July 30th 1975. Angels lost in an array of confusion.

Rambling on

*H*ere's a couple of lines.
This time, they don't mean to rhyme.
Goodbye.

Watched you come and go.
Picture Show. Traveling Show.
Passing time. Passing through.
Back on the dusty road.

Each time, wonder how much to care.
Seems to slip off somewhere.
But the rings once exchanged
Seem to be only reminders
Of short-term wanderings.

Watch the lines
Stream across the page.
And collect them all
In a folder of Traveling Days.

Should I write a poem that says it all
Or should I just keep rambling.
Ramble across the lonely road.

#589 August 2nd 1975. Another goodbye, again. Now, collected in this folder of Traveling Days.

This time around, again

So many more lines
  Just a space and a summer away.

Sat and talked about the seasons

And how they come fading

Into memories once believed.

Writing a line to myself

Shifting thoughts in between.

Passing time, passing through.

Still on the run

In search of the sun.

Wonder what else will be new.

So many more lines

Have yet to be written

So many circles yet to spin.

And it was another welcome back.

Three times around again.

Smoking starry daydreams

Wandering back and forth inside.

Poems to read while on the road, across the highway.

Wherever you are. Wherever you go.

Poems to be where you are.

This time. Around again.

#590 August 2nd 1975. The returning winds bring a change of seasons for the third time this year.

Seasons in my home

Winter,

Spring,

Summer,

Fall.

The seasons spin around this year.

Winter came like a stranger in the night.

And brought a chill to the day.

She wasn't very happy.

She went on her way.

Spring is like a flower, given to me.

But so far away from my soul.

She is the best season for me.

She even let me know.

Summer keeps coming around the corner.

Midnight surprises in silhouettes.

She never stays long enough

Except for her cigarettes.

Fall changes colors, inside and out.

One of the best they could be.

She lost the road I've been searching for.

She was more than a dream.

And other thoughts.
My mind wanders.
Wherever else to do.

Sometimes I wonder
What I'm looking for.
And then I find,
Seasons in my home.

#591 August 3rd 1975. I thought the seasons had sorted themselves out by now.
Clip art of fishing for mermaids in a violent ocean on a clear night.

Wondering Why

*S*at at the table to write a poem
    To write a couple of lines.
    Wondering why it's summer.
Wondering why this time.

If you want to dance
You got to play the music.
What is the tune for the player to play?

Sat outside this evening
To space more time away.
To put my dreams in a cloud.
Wondering why I'm sitting here, wondering why.

Spending my time like nickels and dimes.
A number that dances in my head.
Wondering why I don't have the time this time.
Then space my dreams away.

I don't have the time to be spending my time
To waste it all away.
When it lets me down it is because now
It is only the reason why.

#593 August 4th 1975. Wondering why I am still wandering. Wait, someone's knocking at the door.

More bright lights

*W*ell, she said, "Here I am once again.
Another page to my story.
So many miles having to travel
To start from scratch again."

Bright lights and promises
Bound across the corner, hidden across the page.
She looked at the calendar passing so many days.

She took to the highway in search of a dream.
With no strings to bind her or to find a reason for being.

So many miles to cover another lonely town.
Rainbows in her pocket
Reaching high and chasing
All of her dreams around.

She rode in the clouds that fogged her view
Something she said she'll never do.

And looking for an answer
To fill her empty soul
No excuses to carry her way. Nowhere else to go.

She rode in the clouds
And the highway
By my way.

So many times I was one step behind
Picking up the pieces of her shattered life.

I've watched you chase the rainbows in search of the sun
That seemed so far away.
And like an angel without wings
Trying to touch the sky. You tripped and fell instead.

Yet, chasing through your mind
You seem to find all the dreams that got away.
Spinning around in circles
To reach the ground
You watched the rainbows fade.

The lady was a traveler
Who love the open road.
She carried her dreams in her pocket
She thought was filled with gold.

Letters and lines across the page
Across the highway
She told her story
Another line
Why she had to leave.

#594 August 5th 1975. She was back again. And then she left again.

Always a goodbye

*S*herry left today.
    Kathy comes tomorrow.
      Keli said hello again.
Janice stopped on by.
Beth is gone away.

Another day.
Another line.
Always, another goodbye.

Another hello
Travels in circles.
Nice to hear the silence for awhile.

And a season of dreams constantly spinning
Always seems to be another goodbye.

Just a couple of thoughts to let you know I'm here.
Just a couple of lines
To let you know I still care.

#597 August 18, 1975. There are only so many times and so many lines.
A bouquet of flowers from Sherry before she left. Years later, Keli told me she died of an overdose at age 28.

Summer is gone

A spiral that spins in
And goes out again.
Like a circled web weaved to hold.
Like summertime rambling
And silhouettes of gold
That passed on through the seasons.

The summer is gone
Like it never had come
Except in a pipe filled dream
That keeps bringing stories
That keeps forming scenes
They keep bringing rhymes to me.

Collecting my books to get back to school.
Summer was the season that passed on by.
Only stayed for short time.
That's fine. I've spaced my time.

#598 August 25th 1975. Time to collect my thoughts and my schoolbooks while others traveled on.

Weekend retreat

R eading over lines on a mystical weekend retreat.
The fire crackles softly by our makeshift beds.

Whispering wind at the door. The stubborn trees in the way.

Rain drops on the rooftop. Clouds cover the cabin.

Flames dancing. Shadows against the walls

Blowing endlessly with echoing calls.

#600 September 6, 1975. Some of my best times are often forgotten.
Artwork of Kathy at the fireplace, Mt. Lemmon, 1975.

And now, I move forward.

So far from home

W rite a poem
So close to home
Yet, so far away.

Light up and smoke all of the years or just space them away.

Now, I'm leaving you. Doesn't that make you sad?

Now, you're leaving me. Doesn't that bring you shame?

Chase all your troubles into beer and some pills.

Turn your head away.

When your children come looking for you with tears in their eyes.

What you going to say?

You ask where I'm heading.

And why so long, and why so many mistakes on the way?

But look yourself and we'll look at us. Separate and fade.

No one's mistakes.

There's more to say.

But we never had the words.

Can smile at some of the days

That I never seem to know.

Where are you going

Now, that you're on your way?

Or don't you even know.

#601 September 26, 1975. I don't want to make those same mistakes.

Author of my dreams

My lines form from my world
In a stone drawn haze.
My thoughts give life to the dreams I seem to create.

I. THE MAGUS

Rituals from my hand.
Ramblings from my mind.
Wanderings of my hand.
Blank pages filled with lines.

Collected thoughts,
My Book of Spells.
My spirit expresses my soul.
Within myself unconsciously
My implements work my will.
Imagination across the page
State of mind written expressively.

I have created fallen angels
From my pen.

All a part of thoughts in my world.

And for so long I let them fly
Right by the water's coast.

I have created flowers, rainbows, sweet dreams and more.
Across highways in other planes
I was their souvenir.

Written words expressed their dreams and fears.

For all they would show,

I was the guide

Of their Traveling Show.

They came in and stayed for a while.

But, they left when the lines said

It's time for angels to fly.

Ramblings from my head

They brought the world to me.

Now lines express the ramblings

In a brighter word to read.

I'm the author of my dreams.

#602 September 29,1975. Writing lines to spin my dreams, or theirs.
Artwork, The Magus, 1973.

Reflecting

*C*hilly evenings round again.
Waiting for a change.
Sunshine fading, shared the day,
And some time with an old friend.

Been thinking of a smile. More than far away.
Traveling on a rainbow. Sweet dreams another day.

New faces seem to intervene.
Same ones hang around.
Farther than a mirrored stare
Images of circus clowns.

Looking again trying hard to write a poem.
Been so long, it's hard to say
How I feel my thoughts come down.

Magic words they flow along
And stoned ponies gallop away.
Merry go round ups and downs
Another one on the way.

#606 October 15, 1975. So many things have passed me by. Another visitor at the doorstep.
Artwork of pyramid magician, 1977.

Fantasy reality

She traveled so many miles
So many years along the same road.
Spent among the highway
Chasing after rainbows.

Seeking many directions
Speeding fantasies and dreams.
Trying so hard to make rainbows
Out of reflections
Out of what she's really seeing.

She knew the towns by no name
Only by their spinning games.
It was a dreamer's world
To be disguised in reality.

She smiled behind some lines,
Moods she rearranged.
To cover up the memories
Of when it began to rain.

Like traveling in a dream
Reality wasn't there.
Just make believe the floating scenes
Floating in dreams – fantasies
Reality wasn't there.

Playing out the scenes
That traveled on the mind.
Duality – can't you see
One has to be left behind.

Dancing across the stage
If she amuses the people, she smiles.
Backpack and cigarettes
If she closes her eyes, she travels.

#608 November 15th 1975. Been thinking of her - and she calls.

184

Growing flowers

Why do my plants keep dying?

Always seem to give them care.

Gave each one a little sun

Watered the flowers they never gave.

Was it they never cared to grow old?

Flowers sometimes meant an early grave.

Meant to change to something new

Meant to change their ways.

Was the sun too warm for their souls?

Sometimes too much sun

Can be fatal to a growing thing.

Maybe they think they'll be blinded.

Was it too much care that was always there

Until the leaves turned and faded?

Couldn't reach them any other way.

Wanted them to flower someday.

Why do my plants keep dying?

Guess I don't know their game.

Maybe I should stop trying.

Growing flowers can bring such pain.

#609 December 3rd 1975. Sometimes, I use too much water on my plants.

Just always movin' on

A few months later, I saw her knocking on the same front door.
She smiled and she said so sweetly,
"Been chasing the road once more."

Was morning time, which was fine. She said she thought she'd say hello.
Collecting her thoughts and cigarettes. Space some time off the road.

We talked of lines and silhouettes. And the rainbows that never came.
Only could stay awhile with a smile. Time to move on to other ways.

We shared thoughts and memories. Another little space in time.
Got new places and fantasies. Got new words to try and rhyme.
She looked at the stars out on the road. And chased them all in her mind.
And when it came to security
Seems she'd drop on by.

She danced fancy dances. Played the Traveling Shows.
Was a minstrel in the spinning web.
Never had a place to go.

She stopped by for reflections to cast away in a storm.
Chased rainbows into a wall while always movin' on.

She dances fancy tunes with a smile.
Just enough to get her by.
Been sliding, not really trying
Is good enough for her alibi.

But the tears she can never hide
Seem to be deposited by my side.
Been so long on the same road.
Don't know any other way.

She'd write some lines when feeling so far away.
She'd make up some dreams to help her move along her way.
She'd reach for rainbows hoping to make it through another day.

She wants to find the sun, she says.
Though she's been searching the clouds.
Security won't give the sunshine she needs.
Never has time to settle down.

No poems along the highway.
Just thoughts along the way,
Knocking on my front door.
Just to space some time away.
Glad you decided to stop and stay awhile
And tried to smile.

#612 December 9, 1975. It's been another year of chasing rainbows. Welcome back for a while.

Western wind

Beyond the trees follows the horizon
and the trail spotted with snow.
Past the stream that's still frozen.
Beyond the flowers waiting to grow.

Behind the mountains rest the city
and people with no place to go.

Inside dreams that keep on
spacing across the artificial
roads.

The birds keep on singing.
Playing games with no rules to
bend.

Looking to where the sun
keeps on setting.
Flying into the western wind.

#615 February 6, 1976. Or was the wind
blowing east? I keep losing my direction.

Artwork of a barren tree, from a trip up Mt. Lemmon, October 1974.

Canary

It wasn't as though the wind had actually blown through the trees.
Just because the leaves have moved.
Just because it appeared to be.

The branches that reach out to the sun
And the roots scattered
Beneath the ground
Anchor the dreams
Of fruitful days.

Circles. Like a child playing games.
The birds go from tree to tree
Collecting remnants for a nest to build.
Looking for a place to settle home
They never stay too long.
They sing sweet songs from faraway
Asking for another to play.
Where they go and dance a show
They keep an eye out for bait.

Ever listen to a canary sing?
Almost like an actor on the stage
And only in tune when it wants to be.
Free blowing trees, canary in a cage.

#617 April 20th 1976. Thirty years later, a real dove stopped by. All the others flew away.
Artwork of the Lost Bird, drawn January 1976.

On a rock

*O*n a rock at the
Edge of a mountaintop.
Watching the sun slowly slip on by.

Spacing my thoughts across the valley.
Spacing in my mind across the sky.

A chance to do some reflecting.
Been awhile since I stepped inside
And asked myself where I am traveling
Or if I'm just spacing across time.

The daylight spoke in radiating rays
and wrapped around me, whispering.

Like the wind breathing through the trees, racing by my eyes. Glistening.
Wasn't going to climb any higher without some help to get back down.
Been wandering these hills for so damn long.
Time to bring myself on home.

Yet, I get carried away
By another revolving flame
Which keeps me spinning these circles.
Outside, this sky is clear tonight.
Inside, it kind of feels like rain.

#619 May 17th 1976. We all sit on top of our own mountaintops.
Photo with some friends on top of Mt. Lemmon, 1974.

Anachronism

Nightfall, a full moon on the rise.
Standing over the valley
Looking down cliffs and the mountainside.

Eyes weary from daytime
Long time, filled with age.
Wandering, descending
Years and a few days.
Constantly searching
For a soft place to lie.

No mattresses, no waterbeds.
Not even a dream away.
Old man, travel on,
Wear your face full of age.
Growing mind, growing sleepy
Into twilight, where images sway.
Prophets and lunatics
Lead me from water, land and air
And then into space.
Now destroyed, by a bullet
That causes a cloud.
2,000 years ahead of a 1,000 left behind.

#621 June 1976. Feeling stuck in time.

Stardust

*S*tardust and daydreams across the sky.
   Weaving in and out of the darkness
   Like the millions of people spinning their souls
In an out of our lives.

Some that you can reach near by.
Others that space against lines.
Few that let their brightness shine.
Most don't have the time.

Stardust glittering across my mind.
Reflecting against the midday sun.
And shining like memories space away
In the smiles and tears once left behind.

Some which are easy to find.
Galaxies within their mind.
Few which even begin to glow.
Most don't have the time.

#626 July 14, 1976. Written while visiting old friends up north while I played the Traveling Man.

Small town blues

We sat in a downtown small-town rock'n'roll bar.
A thousand miles from anywhere I've known.
Even farther in my mind of any place I've gone.

We talked about the highway,
Cornfields and rolling hills somewhere up north.
Found myself in someone else's dream
That had the memories
Once whispered to me.

We walked down the
avenue of cottonwood trees
and squirrels.

Reflecting the steps through
the stories of small-town
blues.

How they brought her
down. And how she
traveled to the city to make
her dreams come around.

Only to find that it let her
down.

Traveling, common knowledge, to share.

Written across the lines in rhymes
Of a traveler across the rainbows
In search of smiles not painted on walls
But found plastered against the open road.

And a walk on a moonlit eve
Told me time had taken its toll.
And wiped away the star dust
That traveled across my eyes.

It left instead an open highway
Which seemed to be at my feet.
Leading me in another direction
Of more small town dreams to meet.

And shouldn't I have known.
That you can't bring the sun to shine
On a cloudy day.

#627 July 15th 1976. I realize what it's like taking my Traveling Show to someone else's town.
Clip art of a traveler stopping in a town.

Dawn

The dawn broke into a rainbow spray of colors
Reaching across the morning sky.
The sun rose and touched the heavens
Flashing blindness in my eyes.

I wandered down a well worn path
Stepping over stones, I overcame before.
Looking at scenes, that I've already seen
Somewhere in my mind, once more.

When the clouds gather and the rain begins to fall
I find myself trying to find shelter away from it all.
So I won't have to stumble over stones I never knew before.

Angels from heaven guide me along the way.
Some of them go. And some of them stay.
Sometimes too quickly. Just spinning away.

Again, spending my time spread between lines,
A story and another page.

Walking across a running stream.
Whispering songs sung long ago.
Winding myself around rocks, dreams, mountains and trees.
Wandering to find somewhere else to go.

#631 November 1st 1976. Looking back at the reverse sunset. I think it's time to go back home.

In Retrospect

Now that more time has passed, so have the adventures that generated so much prose. It was time to collect my books and move on.

Grey hairs

The sunlight in your eyes has gone away
Covered by the clouds of your own sorrows.
The laughter in your smile has faded.
Grown a bit older like sweet, sour wine.

The wrinkles of lines worn by time
Etched against your weary face.
Tell me the stories you never had told.
Whisper the secret you're afraid to share.

One day, I'll see myself in your reflection
Across the lines of age I'm soon to wear.
And the distance between our breaths
Won't be as far away.

I wish you could, again, touch my heart
With your warm words and gentle care.
I dreamed you had no love for me.
And when I awoke, you weren't there.

#638 February 16th 1977. As I read these poems over 30 years later, the words still echo.

Advice to a traveler

The evening moved past me
>Beside the sparkling stars against the sky.
>Reflecting the moon inside my mind

That shown in the glare of my eyes.

Behind the darkened walls
I traveled the back roads of my mind.
Creating heavens in a deep blue sky.
Naked angels standing side by side.

They traveled along by my side.
Their breaths lead me across the sky.
I awoke to illusions in my eyes.
Journeying in the dark of my mind.

If you awaken in your sleep,
Somewhere, behind your closed eyes.
Travel the low road beneath the sky
Til you're able to ride their side -
Or just find another way.

#639 February 23rd 1977. Every traveler travels their own road. Now, I look back to where I've been.

Candle burning

She spun herself like a web
  Weaving her intricate patterns.
  An Angel dancing around the flame,
Around the flame she spun for me.

Her eyes danced and flamed with fire
As she spun her tales inside of me.
Carrying me along as she pleased
In her fantasies, silently dancing.

She danced around a candle,
Her body swaying to the flame.
She danced in between the shadows,
Dancing fancy across the stage.

As she moved, she whisked me away
Into the flame of the candle burning.
The wax dripped as it melted away
Into the web she spun around me.

And a fancy dance, the dancer does.
Spinning the flame inside me.
When she stopped, the flame had died.
Passed into the candle burning.

#674 March 2nd 1977. 22 going onto 23. Still lighting candles entranced by the flames.

Misty Dawn

*T*he misty dawn
Whispered good morning
To someone so far away.
Sent a little love
And a sunrise smile
To shine upon your day.

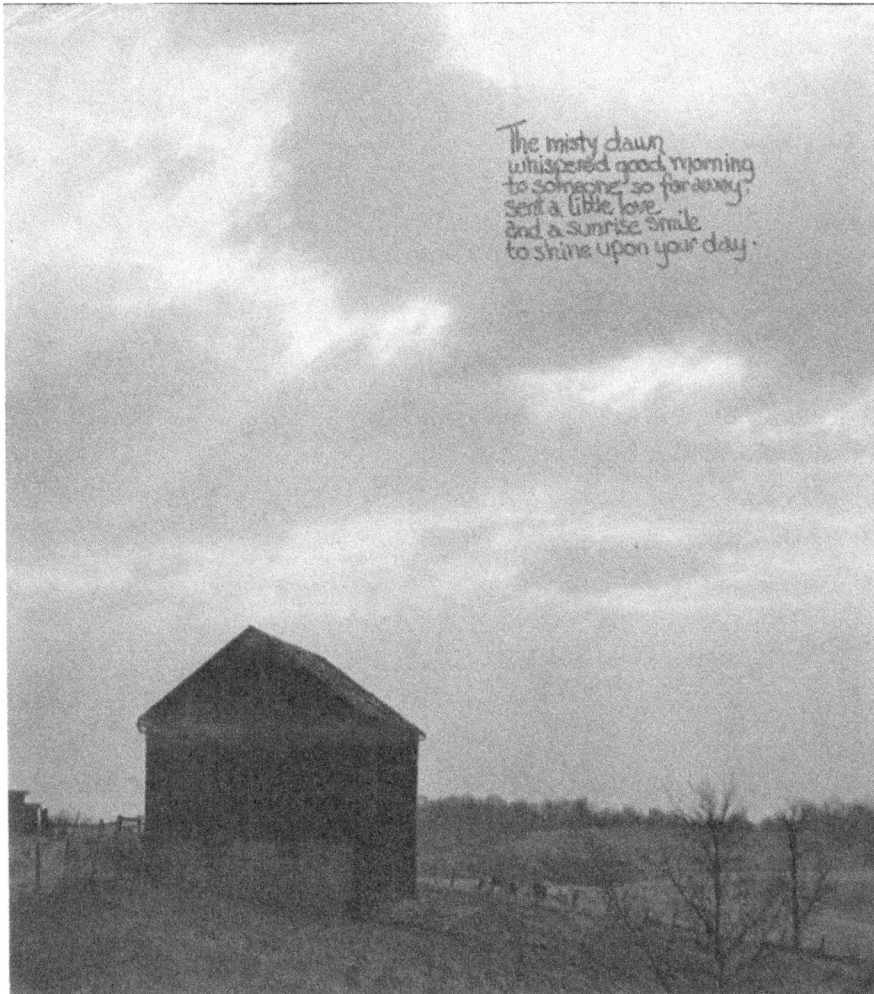

#622 June 23, 1977. A poem mailed to Keli on this card.

Too many times

W hen the time has worn away
From the sands
That have shifted too many times
To ever be the same again.

And when the spirit is drained
From the soul
Taken away too many times
To ever feel the same again.

The rain has fallen
And washed away
The dirt once collected
By the beach.
Now, drained away.

#647 April 2, 1980- just about to turn 26. My fate is sealed a decade after the journey began.

Slipped away

I watched the sunrise pass by my window
As I sat looking out, looking in.
Touched a glimpse of its rays to waken me.
Its heart pounding inside my dreams.

Watched the highway pass over my soul,
And all behind and in front of me.
Searching for a directing road,
Traveling alone, often lonely.

Sweet lights of a midnight city
Calling for me to carry myself home.
Away from what I kept hiding
Slipped on by without even knowing.

#645 October 27, 1980. Where do the days go when no one's looking?

Time slipping away

*G*lanced at the clock, swept the hours away.

It just hadn't seemed that long ago.

Those simple rhymes may have gotten me by.

And I'm still sitting, waiting, for more.

In darkness, somewhere, in between the dreams

Where all of paths seem to be leading

I make my turn without looking back.

Signposts keep sending me astray.

#648 December 2nd 1980. Years pass. My journey continues. Fancy dancers chased other rainbows. Photo taken in the early 1980s, somewhere between Tucson and Phoenix chasing an angel.

K

Your smile shines so bright inside.
It takes me into your company.
Brings me up, when I'm so down
Comforts me when I'm spinning.

Fears, security, both of our tears.
Moments we shared in between
A couple of days turn into years
Always around when needed.

My heart comes too close.
Too many times, too near.
I keep looking at you hiding
Dodging dreams with closed eyes.

And, we wait until the flower wilts.
Borrow time across the winds.
We cross each other's directions
Seeking shelter from the seasons.

We become Guardian Angels
Of each other's souls.
Love too deeply to ever let go.

Both our lives with so many changes.
Hard to cope when going alone.
You look to me when it gets rough.
I turn to you when I need a friend.

Different lives, yet so much the same.
Hard to adjust when passing our ways.
You ask for hope when I take you in.
I share mine when you need a home.

December 4, 1980. For Kaye. She passed away December 3, 2005 – 25 years later almost to the day. Déjà vu. Portrait of Kaye drawn December 23, 1980.

Holiday spirit

I feel like a lonely traveler
Stumbling down this nameless road.
Too cold from too many nights
To high from being so low.

No backpack and no cigarettes.
Just a cloud to cover my soul.
Shattered illusions and spare change.
Watching myself grow old.

The darkness,
The highway,
The chill from winter's snow.
Where am I going?

A clock with no hands.
A song with no tune.
No place to go.

Well, jolly holiday spirit
Who seeps into my bones.
Do more than just get me drunk
Take me home.

#652 December 23rd 1980, now age 26. Looking through the eyes of travelers and seeing myself.

Sunset

I watched the sunset pass by my window as I sat looking out, looking in.
Touched a glimpse of its rays to warm me.
Its heart and feelings inside my dreams.

I watched the highway pass over my soul, all behind and in front of me.

Searching for a directing road and traveling alone.

Sweet lights of a midnight city calling for me to carry myself home.

Away from what I kept hiding slipped on by without knowing.

If I try to break the silence of tears gathering around me,
Will it just be an echo of how I really feel?

When there's no one to share building blocks, love and dreams,
And no place to go. When I feel like running, then, I stop to readjust
And look for a new direction.

October 27, 1980. With the sunset behind me, I can look into the night sky and imagine.
Arizona desert sunset photograph.

Stepping Stones

*W*hen all the people go home
There sits an empty stage.
Played to an audience of thousands
Who doesn't even know their names.

Sounds transformed into vibrations.
And I'm left alone again.
Moving onto another one
When time strikes right again.

I'm only a player
In a Traveling Show.
A musical note.
A stepping stone.
Broken chords.
Broken hearts.

July 3, 1983. Just another stepping stone. Roxy flew away with more than my heart. She passed away August 2010.

Dusty Trail

*I*n my dreams
I have contacts with wanderers
Who lead me astray.

When I'm awake
Some of those wanderers
Become my travelers.

We share a path together
Until other paths split our way
Whether by dream or wake.

July 6, 1983. Old friends appear in dreams and then knock on my door. New ones take their place.

Perpetual motion

Y ou live you life in a perpetual game.
A spinning wheel, its end is its beginning.
You keep on starting over again.
When the chips start to fall,
You always go back for more.

You spend your time on reflections.
Paint by number fantasies
Which lead you in no direction,
Except where you've already been.

And I sit here, watching you
Spin your wheels around again.
Hiding from tomorrow
Because you fear today.
So, you try to revive
Your yesterday.

#655 August 1, 1983. I wrote this for someone else- but it seemed like it was for me.

Advice to a Night Traveler

The evening moves quickly past
Sparking stars against the sky.
Silhouetted imagery plays
Behind closed eyes.

Traveling the back roads
Of night time dreams,

Creating lucid visions
Out of fantasies.

Reality cuts like a knife
When it comes to take you away.
Away from the scenes
That make you want to dream.

Awaken,
To the minds' illusions,
In disguise.

Travel the low roads
'til you can touch the light.

#656 August 1, 1983. See "Advice to A Traveler" (February 1977) – 6 years earlier.

Dust

Swept across the desert
Like dust across a grave.
Looking for a place to settle,
Any place along the way.

Swept across the ocean,
Like dust across the waves.
Searching for a little land
Or island which I can stay.

Stepped across the waters
Flew across the air
Upside down, while inside out.
Sometimes, just nowhere.

Just an attitude.
Shadowed behind
What I want to see.

Just an attitude
Turned around
What I want to be.

#658 June 23, 1991. A year later, another angel flew over the waters and settled for a while.

I ran out of words.

June 1, 2000, age 46. The words became buried with passing time and stored away in boxes for decades.

Midnight inside

*D*ecades pass like water
Flowing beneath the bridge.
So many different currents
Flowing through my mind.

A lifetime gone so long ago
Still alive in between lines.
Halfway between a beacon
And a multitude of signs.

#660 June 9th 2003 at age 49. Remembering those traveling days among piles of letters, photos and poems.

Across the spectrum

ow, spaced across the decades
Fancy dancers have moved on.
If they found their sweet dreams and rainbows
I may never know.

Some have found their way
Above the heavens they once sought.

Some lost their way
In the dreams that they lost.

June 19, 2012 at age 58. That's how their story ends.

Sherry passed away July 1, 1982.

Kaye passed away December 3, 2005.

Beth passed away August 8, 2008.

Roxy passed away August 5, 2010.

A dove in my hand

A dove flies onto my hand
Looking for something
No other bird can satisfy.

A dove does a fancy dance around my feet
Beckoning for me to play
Until it finds its home.

September 22, 2012. Another lost bird finds a temporary home.
Photo of a dove in my hand, September 18, 2012.

*"Then the angel that talked with me went forth, and said unto me,
Lift up now thine eyes, and see what is this that goeth forth."*

Zechariah 5:5

Words Between the Lines

Illustrations

"Traveling on a rainbow

In hopes to reach the sun.

A piece of sky,

A piece of dream.

Angels across the heavens."

#463 November 20, 1974

About the Author

R obert E. Zucker has been a newspaper, book and Internet publisher, journalism instructor and author of dozens of unpublished manuscripts and nearly one thousand poems over the past four decades.

Writing has always been a part of my life. Whether on paper or digital, my life has been recorded in words. These poems are part of that journey.

After penning the bulk of these lines, in 1978, I launched Tucson, Arizona's first newspaper published for and by local youth that evolved, a decade later into the *Entertainment Magazine*. The print publishing phase ended when it became one of Arizona's first newspapers to publish online in January 1995 as EMOL.org- *Entertainment Magazine On Line*.

Teaching courses and maintaining the computer labs for the University of Arizona's Department of Journalism and Pima Community College's Media Communications Department also filled the years between 1992 and 2005. That's when the Internet began to emerge as a viable way to make living and I could return to publishing in 2005- without the newsprint.

Besides compiling hundreds of poems over several decades, there are piles of unfinished fiction books to edit and filing cabinets of research on parapsychology still waiting.

These poems and my artwork, created between 1969 and 2000, tell my story in prose from high school through college and beyond. As the poems evolved, they strung together a storyline of the lives of the people who passed through my life. While the poems may have special meaning to me, and evoke strong memories of those days gone by, those same words can echo a memory in almost anyone's life. This book took 40 years to live and write. Now, as I look back at the piles of letters, photographs and poems, I revealed my own Traveling Show.

Robert Zucker

Photo taken at Rocky Point, Mexico, 2009

Clip art from the Zedcor, Inc. DeskGallery image collection, 1994 and public domain sources.

I'm only a poem.

A poem I'm meant to be.

And as a poem

I'm the story of me.

#472 December 31, 1974

www.ingramcontent.com/pod-product-compliance
Lightning Source LLC
LaVergne TN
LVHW081332060426
835513LV00014B/1261